"Every now and then, somebody needs to step on the toes of the body of Christ. Reading this book may make you wince, but the pain of self-examination is worth it. Take it to your pastor. To your small group. To your Sunday school teacher. Urge them to take up these serious challenges and wake the church to the demands of discipleship."

David Neff, editor & vice president, *Christianity Today*

"In the thirty years since Ron Sider seared the conscience of evangelicals with the publication of *Rich Christians in an Age of Hunger*, evangelicalism in North America has lost whatever claim it had to being a counterculture. *The Scandal of the Evangelical Conscience* summons us, once again, to take the gospel seriously. For the good of society—and perhaps even for the sake of our souls—we had better take notice."

Randall Balmer, author, *Growing Pains:
Learning to Love My Father's Faith*

"When the behavior of members of a religious movement turns out to be little better, and sometimes worse, than that of its neighbors, leaders and members of that movement should take notice. They should ask some deep questions not only about that behavior but also about the systems that produce or support it. Ron Sider has me asking those kinds of questions, thanks to his clear diagnosis and thoughtful prescription in *The Scandal of the Evangelical Conscience*."

Brian McLaren, pastor, author

"If you've ever wondered why today's evangelicals lack the societal influence their numbers would seem to bestow, Ron Sider offers an answer in *The Scandal of the Evangelical Conscience*. Quibble with him here and there as we might, but until the evangelical church is willing to face the biblical issues Sider raises, I fear we will continue to find our cultural saltiness leaching away."

Duane Litfin, president, Wheaton College

"Ron Sider's greatest gift to the church is his willingness to tell us the hard, obvious truth about ourselves. This book is strong medicine—a diagnosis that will take your breath away, but also a prescription that

D0981323

could make the difference between life and death for biblical faith in America."

Andy Crouch, former editor of *Re:generation Quarterly*

"Written by a scholar who believes the biblical gospel and loves the evangelical church, this book is a powerful protest against cheap grace and a call to faithful discipleship. Like Carl Henry's *Uneasy Conscience* a half-century ago, may Ron Sider's *Scandal of the Evangelical Conscience* nudge us out of our complacency."

Timothy George, dean, Beeson Divinity School of Samford University; executive editor, *Christianity Today*

"The conscience of many evangelicals has been programmed more by social patterns than by Scripture. In this work Ron Sider gives us an impressive critique of this scandal and calls us to a rediscovery of the ethics of Christ. This book can help us see that being saved in relation with Jesus means that we now live in relation with Jesus. The church is the body of Christ, the community that makes Jesus visible in the world. Our ability to be self-critical is in itself an evidence of the sincerity of our faith. This book is a call to repentance and renewal."

Myron S. Augsburger, president emeritus, Eastern Mennonite University; president emeritus, Council for Christian Colleges & Universities

"'Scandal' is not too strong a word for the shortfall in holy living among us evangelicals. Ron Sider has forcefully articulated what other Christian leaders have begun to identify as a 'crisis'—a crisis of Christology—a crisis in how we see, seek, speak about, and serve God's Son for *all* that he is. While laying before us convincing evidences of the spiritual impotency and paralysis of our lives and churches, Sider infuses us with great hope that, by a more consistent embrace of the lordship of Jesus, the evangelical movement can once again impact the world around us 'in a manner worthy of the Lord' (Eph. 4:1)."

David Bryant, founder, PROCLAIM HOPE!; author, *Christ Is All! A Joyful Manifesto on the Supremacy of God's Son*

THE SCANDAL OF THE EVANGELICAL CONSCIENCE

WHY ARE
CHRISTIANS
LIVING JUST LIKE
THE REST
OF THE WORLD?

RONALD J. SIDER

BakerBooks
Grand Rapids, Michigan

Published by Baker Books
a division of Baker Publishing Group
P.O. Box 6287, Grand Rapids, MI 49516-6287
www.bakerbooks.com

Sixth printing, November 2006

Printed in the United States of America

Library of Congress Cataloging-in-Publication Data
Sider, Ronald J.
    The scandal of the evangelical conscience : why are Christians living just like the rest of the world? / Ronald J. Sider.
        p.   cm.
    Includes bibliographical references.
    ISBN 10: 0-8010-6541-0
    ISBN 978-0-8010-6541-5
    1. Evangelicalism—United States. 2. Church and the world. I. Title.
BR1642.U5S458 2005
277.3′083—dc22   2004022340

In memory of my mother and father
Ida and James Sider
who lived what they preached

Contents

Acknowledgments

Without my former student Brent D. Miller, this book probably would not have been written. The basic concept tumbled around in my mind for several years. But the project began to move only when Brent wrote a long, excellent research paper laying out much of the statistical data that I use in chapter 1. Later, when I finally decided to write the book, Brent gladly agreed to do further research. Two other graduate students, Robin Weinstein and Chris Klopp, also provided valuable help.

As in all my writing projects over the past twenty years, my administrative assistant, Naomi Miller, has provided outstanding support. A special thanks to all the folk who make possible the ministry of Evangelicals for Social Action and the Sider Center on Ministry and Public Policy at Eastern Seminary, and finally to all my colleagues at Eastern Seminary and Eastern University, institutions that continue to provide a wonderful home for all my work.

Introduction

Once upon a time there was a great religion that over the centuries had spread all over the world. But in those lands where it had existed for the longest time, its adherents slowly grew complacent, lukewarm, and skeptical. Indeed, many of the leaders of its oldest groups even publicly rejected some of the religion's most basic beliefs.

In response, a renewal movement emerged, passionately championing the historic claims of the old religion and eagerly inviting unbelievers everywhere to embrace the ancient faith. Rejecting the skepticism of leaders who no longer believed in a God who works miracles, members of the renewal movement vigorously argued that their God not only had performed miraculous deeds in the past but still miraculously transforms all who believe. Indeed, a radical, miraculous "new birth" that began a lifetime of sweeping moral renewal and transformation was at the center of their preaching. Over time, the renewal movement flourished to the point of becoming one of the most influential wings of the whole religion.

Not surprisingly, the movement's numbers translated into political influence. And the renewal movement was so confident of its beliefs and claims that it persuaded the nation's top political leader to have the government work more closely with religious social service organizations to solve the nation's horrendous social problems. Members of the renewal movement knew that miraculous moral transformation of character frequently happened when broken persons embraced the great religion. They also lobbied politicians to strengthen the traditional definition of marriage because their ancient texts taught that a lifelong covenant between a man and a woman was at the center of the Creator's design for the family.

Then the pollsters started conducting scientific polls of the general population. In spite of the renewal movement's proud claims to miraculous transformation, the polls showed that members of the movement divorced their spouses just as often as their secular neighbors. They beat their wives as often as their neighbors. They were almost as materialistic and even more racist than their pagan friends. The hard-core skeptics smiled in cynical amusement at this blatant hypocrisy. The general population was puzzled and disgusted. Many of the renewal movement's leaders simply stepped up the tempo of their now enormously successful, highly sophisticated promotional programs. Others wept.

This, alas, is roughly the situation of Western or at least American evangelicalism today.

Scandalous behavior is rapidly destroying American Christianity. By their daily activity, most "Christians" regularly commit treason. With their mouths they claim that Jesus is Lord, but with their actions they demonstrate allegiance to money, sex, and self-fulfillment.

The findings in numerous national polls conducted by highly respected pollsters like The Gallup Organization and The Barna Group are simply shocking. "Gallup and Barna," laments evangelical theologian Michael Horton, "hand us survey after survey demonstrating that evangelical Christians are as likely to embrace lifestyles every bit as hedonistic, materialistic, self-centered, and sexually immoral as the world in general."[1] Divorce is *more* common among "born-again" Christians than in the general American population. Only 6 percent of evangelicals tithe. White evangelicals are the *most* likely people to object to neighbors of another race. Josh McDowell has pointed out that the sexual promiscuity of evangelical youth is only a little less outrageous than that of their nonevangelical peers.

Alan Wolfe, famous contemporary scholar and director of the Boisi Center for Religion and American Public Life, has just published a penetrating study of American religious life. Evangelicals figure prominently in his book. His evaluation? Today's evangelicalism, Wolfe says, exhibits "so strong a desire to copy the culture of hotel chains and popular music that it loses what religious distinctiveness it once had."[2] Wolfe argues, "The truth is there is increasingly little difference between an essentially secular activity like the popular entertainment industry and the bring-'em-in-at-any-cost efforts of evangelical megachurches."[3]

It is not surprising that George Barna concludes, "Every day, the church is becoming more like the world it allegedly seeks to change."[4] We have very little time, he believes, to reverse these trends. African Christian and famous missions scholar Professor Lamin Sanneh told *Christianity Today* recently that "the cultural captivity of Christianity in the West is nearly complete, and with the religion tamed, it is open season on the West's Christian heritage. I worry about a West without a moral center facing a politically resurgent Islam."[5]

Our first concern, of course, must be internal integrity, not external danger. What a tragedy for evangelicals to declare proudly that personal conversion and new birth in Christ are at the center of their faith and then to defy biblical moral standards by living almost as sinfully as their pagan neighbors.

Graham Cyster, a Christian whom I know from South Africa, recently told me a painful story about a personal experience two decades ago when he was struggling against apartheid as a young South African evangelical. One night, he was smuggled into an underground Communist cell of young people fighting apartheid. "Tell us about the gospel of Jesus Christ," they asked, half hoping for an alternative to the violent communist strategy they were embracing.

Graham gave a clear, powerful presentation of the gospel, showing how personal faith in Christ wonderfully transforms persons and creates one new body of believers where there is neither Jew nor Greek, male nor female, rich nor poor, black nor white. The youth were fascinated. One seventeen-year-old exclaimed, "That is wonderful! Show me where I can see that happening." Graham's face fell as he sadly responded that he could not think of anywhere South African Christians were truly living out the message of the gospel. "Then the whole thing is a piece of sh—," the youth angrily retorted. Within a month he left the country to join the armed struggle against apartheid—eventually giving his life for his beliefs.

The young man was right. If Christians do not live what they preach, the whole thing is a farce. "American Christianity has largely failed since the middle of the twentieth century," Barna concludes, "because Jesus' modern-day disciples do not act like Jesus."[6] This scandalous behavior mocks Christ, undermines evangelism, and destroys Christian credibility.

If vital Christian faith is to survive, we must understand the depth of the crisis, discover why it has happened, and develop obedient, faithful correctives. That is what this book seeks to do. Chapter 1 lays out the extent of the scandal. Chapter 2 contrasts our disobedience with the biblical teaching about the wonderful, transforming, sanctifying power of genuine faith in and union with Christ. Chapters 3 and 4 explore the root causes of this scandal and the biblical foundations that can correct it. Finally, chapter 5 points to some rays of hope. My prayer is that just as Mark Noll's book *The Scandal of the Evangelical Mind* contributed so much to strengthen evangelical thinking, so too this book will renew evangelical resolve to live what we preach.

The Depth of the Scandal

Evangelical Christians are as likely to embrace lifestyles every bit as hedonistic, materialistic, self-centered, and sexually immoral as the world in general.

Michael Horton

How bad are things? What is the depth of the scandal? Unless we face these questions with ruthless honesty, we can never hope to correct things.

Whether the issue is divorce, materialism, sexual promiscuity, racism, physical abuse in marriage, or neglect of a biblical worldview, the polling data point to widespread, blatant disobedience of clear biblical moral demands on the part of people who allegedly are evangelical, born-again Christians. The statistics are devastating.

Divorce

In a 1999 national survey, George Barna found that the percentage of born-again Christians who had experienced divorce was slightly *higher* (26 percent) than that of non-Christians (22 percent).[1] In Barna's polls since the mid-1990s, that number has remained about the same.[2] In August 2001, a new poll found that the divorce rate was about the same for born-again Christians and the population as a whole; 33 percent of all born-again Christians had been divorced compared with 34 percent of non-born-again Americans—a statistically insignificant difference. Barna also found in one study that 90 percent of all divorced born-again folk divorced *after* they accepted Christ.[3]

Barna makes a distinction between born-again Christians and evangelicals. Barna classifies as born-again all who say "they have made a personal commitment to Jesus Christ that is still important in their life today" and who also indicate that they "believe that when they die they will go to heaven because they have confessed their sins and accepted Jesus Christ as their Savior."[4] In Barna's polls anywhere from 35 to 43 percent of the total U.S. population meet these criteria for being born-again.

Barna limits the term "evangelical" to a much smaller group—just 7 to 8 percent of the total U.S. population. In addition to meeting the criteria for being born-again, evangelicals must agree with several other things such as the following: Jesus lived a sinless life; eternal salvation is only through grace, not works; Christians have a personal responsibility to evangelize non-Christians; Satan exists.

Obviously this definition identifies a much more theologically biblical, orthodox group of Christians.

What is the divorce rate among evangelicals? According to a 1999 poll by Barna, exactly the same as the national average! According to that poll, 25 percent of evangelicals—just like 25 percent of the total population—have gone through a divorce.[5] Does it make no difference to evangelicals that their Lord and Savior explicitly, clearly, repeatedly condemned divorce?

> "Have you not read that the one who made them at the beginning 'made them male and female,' and said, 'For this reason a man shall leave his father and mother and be joined to his wife, and the two shall become one flesh'? So they are no longer two, but one flesh. Therefore what God has joined together, let no one separate."
>
> Matthew 19:4–6 NRSV

Professor Brad Wilcox is a Princeton-trained, Christian sociologist who specializes in family issues. Wilcox has studied two sets of national data: *The General Social Survey* and *The National Survey of Families and Households*. The result? "Compared with the rest of the population, conservative Protestants are *more* likely to divorce." He also points out the divorce rates are higher in the southern United States, where conservative Protestants make up a higher percentage of the population than elsewhere in the country.[6]

A story in the *New York Times* in 2001 underlined Wilcox's findings about the unusually high divorce rates in the South. In many parts of the Bible Belt, the divorce rate was discovered to be "roughly 50 percent *above* the national average" (italics mine).[7] Governor Frank Keating of Oklahoma pointed out the irony that these unusually high divorce rates exist in his state, where 70 percent of the people go to church once a week or more. "These divorce rates," Gov. Keating concluded, "are a scalding indictment of what *isn't* being said behind the pulpit."

Materialism and the Poor

John and Sylvia Ronsvalle have been carefully analyzing the giving patterns of American Christians for well over three decades. Their annual *The State of Christian Giving* is the most accurate report for learning how much Christians in the richest nation in human history actually give. In their most recent edition, they provide detailed information about per-member giving patterns of U.S. church members from 1968 to 2001. Over those thirty-plus years, of course, the average income of U.S. Christians has increased enormously. But that did not carry over into their giving. The report showed that the richer we become, the less we give in proportion to our incomes.

In 1968, the average church member gave 3.1 percent of their income—less than a third of a tithe. That figure dropped every year through 1990 and then recovered slightly to 2.66 percent—about one quarter of a tithe.[8]

Even more interesting is what has happened to evangelical giving. The Ronsvalles compare the giving in seven typical mainline denominations (affiliated with the National Council of Churches) with the giving in eight evangelical denominations (with membership in the National Association of

Evangelicals). In 1968 the eight evangelical denomin.
gave considerably more than the seven mainline denominations. While the mainline denominational members gave
3.3 percent of their income, evangelicals gave 6.15 percent.
While this is significantly more, the evangelicals on average
still gave less than two-thirds of a tithe. By 1985 mainline
folk had dropped their giving to 2.85 percent of their income
and evangelicals to 4.74 percent. By 2001, mainline members
had recovered slightly to 3.17 percent, but evangelical giving
kept dropping and was at a mere 4.27 percent.[9]

As we got richer and richer, evangelicals chose to spend
more and more on themselves and give a smaller and smaller
percentage to the church. Today, on average, evangelicals in
the United States give about two-fifths of a tithe.

In 2002, Barna discovered that only 6 percent of born-
again adults tithed—a 50-percent decline from 2000 when
12 percent did. And in 2002, just 9 percent of Barna's narrow
class of evangelicals tithed.[10]

One can see a related problem in another area. Examine
the public agenda of prominent evangelical political movements and coalitions. Virtually never does justice for the
poor appear as an area of significant concern and effort.

American Christians live in the richest nation on earth
and enjoy an average household income of $42,409.[11] The
World Bank reports that 1.2 billion of the world's poorest
people try to survive on just one dollar a day. At least one
billion people have never heard the gospel. The Ronsvalles
point out that if American Christians just tithed, they would
have another $143 billion available to empower the poor
and spread the gospel.[12] Studies by the United Nations suggest that just an additional $70–$80 billion a year would

be enough to provide access to essential services like basic health care and education for all the poor of the earth.[13] If they did no more than tithe, American Christians would have the *private* dollars to foot this entire bill and still have $60–$70 billion more to do evangelism around the world.

As evangelicals we claim to embrace the Bible as our final authority. One of the most common themes in the Scriptures is that God and his faithful people have a special concern for the poor. Why this blatant contradiction between belief and practice?

In the late 1970s, I attended a national conference of evangelical leaders. My small group, as I recall, included prominent persons like Carl Henry, the first editor of *Christianity Today*; Hudson Armerding, the president of Wheaton College; and Loren Cunningham, the founder of Youth with a Mission. Several times in our small group, different persons referred to the issue of a simple lifestyle, urging its importance. Finally, Loren Cunningham said something like the following: "Yes, I think the evangelical community is ready to live more simply—if we evangelical leaders will model it." That ended the discussion. There were no further recommendations to live more simply!

Sexual Disobedience

A story in the *New York Times* reported that, according to census data, in the 1990s the number of unmarried couples living together jumped a lot more in the Bible Belt (where a higher percentage of the total population are evangelicals) than in the nation as a whole. Nationwide, the increase was

72 percent. But in Oklahoma it was 97 percent, in Arkansas 125 percent, and in Tennessee 123 percent.[14]

Popular evangelical speaker Josh McDowell has been observing and speaking to evangelical youth for several decades. I remember him saying years ago that evangelical youth are only about 10 percent less likely to engage in premarital sex than nonevangelicals.

True Love Waits, a program sponsored by the Southern Baptist Convention, is one of the most famous evangelical efforts to reduce premarital sexual activity among our youth. Since 1993, about 2.4 million young people have signed a pledge to wait until marriage to engage in sexual intercourse. Are these young evangelicals keeping their pledges? In March 2004, researchers from Columbia University and Yale University reported on their findings. For seven years they studied twelve thousand teenagers who took the pledge. Sadly, they found that 88 percent of these pledgers reported having sexual intercourse before marriage; just 12 percent kept their promise. The researchers also found that the rates for having sexually transmitted diseases "were almost identical for the teenagers who took pledges and those who did not."[15]

Barna found from a 2001 poll that the rate of cohabitation—living with a member of the opposite sex without marriage—is only a little lower among born-again adults than the general public. Nationally, 33 percent of all adults have lived with a member of the opposite sex without being married. The rate is 25 percent for born-again folk.[16]

Professor John C. Green is an evangelical political scientist and director of the Ray C. Bliss Institute of Applied Politics at the University of Akron. Green is one of the best statisticians in his field and has studied how Americans feel about morals and ethics using several national surveys. He divides those he labels evangelicals into two categories: traditional evangelicals (who have higher church attendance, a higher view of biblical authority, etc.) and nontraditional evangelicals.[17] What are their attitudes on premarital and extramarital sex? Fully 26 percent of traditional evangelicals do *not* think premarital sex is wrong, and 46 percent of nontraditional evangelicals say it is morally okay.[18]

And extramarital sex? Of traditional evangelicals, 13 percent say it is okay for married persons to have sex with someone other than one's spouse. And 19 percent of nontraditional evangelicals say adultery is morally acceptable.[19] Fortunately, Green finds that evangelicals fare better than mainline Protestant and Catholic Christians on these issues, but the number of evangelicals that blatantly reject biblical sexual norms is astonishing.

What about pornography? Citing a recent survey in *Leadership* magazine, Steve Gallagher says, "Tragically, the percentage of Christian men involved [in pornography] is not much different that that of the unsaved."[20]

Racism

In 1989 George Gallup Jr. and James Castelli published the results of a survey to determine which groups in the United States were least and most likely to object to having black neighbors—surely a good measure of racism. Catholics and nonevangelical Christians ranked least likely to object to black neighbors; 11 percent objected. Mainline Protestants came next at 16 percent. At 17 percent, Baptists and evangelicals were among the most likely groups to object to black neighbors, and 20 percent of Southern Baptists objected to black neighbors.[21]

It is common knowledge that during the civil rights movement, when mainline Protestants and Jews joined African Americans in their historic struggle for freedom and equality, evangelical leaders were almost entirely absent. Some opposed the movement; others said nothing. When Frank Gaebelein, then a coeditor of *Christianity Today*, not only covered Martin Luther King's march on Selma but also endorsed and joined the movement, he experienced opposition and hostility from other evangelical leaders.[22] My own school, Eastern Baptist Theological Seminary, was founded in 1925 as an evangelical alternative to theological liberalism in American Baptist circles. But racism was part of our early history. We always accepted African Americans as students but refused to allow African American men to sleep overnight on campus. One African American student, who much later was elected to the seminary's board of trustees, had to sleep five miles away at Thirtieth Street Train Station. Thank God for Cuthbert Rutenber who helped the seminary abandon its racist policies in about 1950.

More recently, evangelicals have taken several important steps to confess past racism and call for change. Coach Bill McCartney, the founder of the national evangelical men's movement called Promise Keepers, was one of the outstanding evangelical leaders in this change. McCartney went on a national speaking tour, regularly calling evangelicals to racial reconciliation. In his book *Sold Out*, McCartney recalls what happened. When he finished speaking, he reports,

"There was no response—nothing. . . . In city after city, in church after church, it was the same story—wild enthusiasm while I was being introduced, followed by a morgue-like chill as I stepped away from the microphone."[23] McCartney thinks a major reason attendance dropped dramatically in Promise Keepers' stadium events was their stand on racial reconciliation.

Michael O. Emerson and Christian Smith have written a crucial book, *Divided by Faith: Evangelical Religion and the Problem of Race in America*, exploring ongoing racial attitudes in the evangelical world. Their conclusion? "White evangelicalism likely does more to perpetuate the racialized society than to reduce it."[24] White conservative Protestants are more than twice as likely as other whites to blame lack of equality (e.g., income) between blacks and whites on a lack of black motivation rather than discrimination. Conservative Protestants are six times more likely to cite lack of motivation than unequal access to education![25]

Evangelicals may have some good biblical theology about the body of Christ, where there is neither Jew nor Greek, black nor white. But if they do not work out this theology in practice, such that white evangelicals welcome black neighbors and work to end racist structures, then, as was made clear by the young South African Communist, the whole thing stinks.

Physical Abuse in Marriage

More than one study has found that women are more likely to experience physical abuse in traditional marriages (where the husband is dominant) than in egalitarian marriages. Evangelicals disagree over whether the Bible supports a traditional or an egalitarian marriage.[26] But it is almost certainly the case that a higher percentage of evangelicals than the general public live in traditional marriages. So where are wives more likely to be beaten?

One important study found that less than "3 percent of wives in egalitarian marriages had been beaten by their husbands in the previous year. In traditional marriages where the husband was dominant, 10.7 percent of wives had been beaten—a rate of violence more than 300 percent higher than for egalitarian marriages."[27] Another study that included over twenty thousand married couples found similar results. In this study, spousal abuse was 400 percent higher in traditional marriages.[28]

A different study found that husbands who attended conservative Protestant churches or held conservative theological views were no more or less likely to engage in domestic abuse than others.[29] And a large study of the Christian Reformed Church (a member of the National Association of Evangelicals) discovered that the frequency of physical and sexual abuse in this evangelical denomination was about the same as in the general population.[30] Theologically conservative Christians, according to these studies, commit domestic abuse at least as often as the general public.

Conclusion

To say there is a crisis of disobedience in the evangelical world today is to dangerously understate the problem. Born-again Christians divorce at about the same rate as everyone else. Self-centered materialism is seducing evangelicals and rapidly destroying our earlier, slightly more generous giving. Only 6 percent of born-again Christians tithe. Born-again Christians justify and engage in sexual promiscuity (both premarital sex and adultery) at astonishing rates. Racism and perhaps physical abuse of wives seem to be worse in evangelical circles than elsewhere. This is scandalous behavior for people who claim to be born-again by the Holy Spirit and to enjoy the very presence of the Risen Lord in their lives.

In light of the foregoing statistics, it is not surprising that born-again Christians spend seven times more hours each week in front of their televisions than they spend in Bible reading, prayer, and worship.[31] Only 9 percent of born-again adults and 2 percent of born-again teenagers have a biblical worldview.[32]

Perhaps it is not surprising either that non-Christians have a very negative view of evangelicals. In a recent poll, Barna asked non-Christians about their attitudes toward different groups of Christians. Only 44 percent have a positive view of Christian clergy. Just 32 percent have a positive view of born-again Christians. And a mere 22 percent have a positive view of evangelicals.[33]

Lest everything seem hopeless, I want to end this sad chapter with one hopeful finding. As we shall see in chapter 5, when we can use more precise measures of faith and distinguish more carefully between deeply committed Christians and others, the statistics on behavior improve significantly. But this hopeful item does not reverse the tragedy of widespread, scandalous disobedience among those who call themselves evangelicals.

28

Evangelicals rightly rejected theological liberalism because it denied the miraculous. In response, we insisted miracles were central to biblical faith at numerous points including the supernatural moral transformation of broken sinners. Now our very lifestyle as evangelicals is a ringing practical denial of the miraculous in our lives. Satan must laugh in sneerful derision. God's people can only weep.

The Biblical Vision

Those who abide in me and I in them bear much fruit.

John 15:5 NRSV

You have been set free from sin and have become slaves to righteousness.

Romans 6:18

No one who is born of God will continue to sin.

1 John 3:9

The contrast between contemporary Christian behavior and New Testament teaching and practice is stark. The extent of our scandalous failure today becomes clear only when we recall what Jesus expected and the early Christians experienced. Jesus called for costly obedience and radical discipleship. In spite of some glaring failures, the early Christians lived profoundly transformed lifestyles. The astonishing quality of their lives attracted people to Christ. Today, our hypocrisy often drives unbelievers away.

In this chapter we take a quick journey through the New Testament. What did Jesus say his disciples would be like? What does the New Testament tell us about what the first Christians thought and how they lived?

The Gospels

Jesus certainly welcomed and forgave sinners. Parable after parable makes this wondrously clear. "I have not come to call the righteous, but sinners," Jesus reminded the Pharisees who disliked Jesus's warm embrace of sinners (Matt. 9:13).

But that does not mean Jesus expected these forgiven sinners to continue in sin. "Go and sin no more," Jesus told the adulterous woman whom the Pharisees wanted to stone and Jesus gladly forgave. Obedience is essential. Not everyone who cries "Lord, Lord" will enter the kingdom, Jesus said, "but only the one who does the will of my Father in heaven" (Matt. 7:21 NRSV).

Jesus summoned his disciples to costly obedience. "If any want to become my followers," he said, "let them deny themselves and take up their cross and follow me. For those who want to save their life will lose it, and those who lose their life for my sake and for the sake of the Gospel will save it" (Mark 8:34–35 NRSV). At another time he insisted that whoever "does not hate father and mother, wife and children, brothers and sisters, yes, and even life itself, cannot be my disciple" (Luke 14:26 NRSV). Jesus was obviously using Hebraic hyperbole. He displayed his own loving concern for his mother as he hung dying on the cross. He did not want his disciples literally to hate or neglect their families. But he certainly did mean to reject in the most unambiguous terms the kind of lukewarm faith and dual loyalty that so many Christians display today. Jesus must be first in our lives, or we are blatantly defying our Lord.

Jesus expected his disciples to forgive others just as he had forgiven them. Again and again he insisted that "if you do not forgive others their trespasses, neither will your Father forgive your trespasses" (Matt. 6:15). In fact, in the Lord's Prayer, Jesus teaches his disciples to pray regularly: "Forgive us our debts, as we also have forgiven our debtors" (Matt. 6:12). And in the stunning parable of the unmerciful servant, the master forgives a huge debt owed by his servant. But when this servant refuses to show the same mercy to one of his tiny debtors, the master angrily retracts his pardon and throws the rascal in prison. Jesus's commentary on the story is blunt: "So my heavenly Father will also do to every one of you, if you do not forgive your brother or sister from your heart" (Matt. 18:35 NRSV).

Jesus knew that his followers would live so differently from the surrounding society that the world would hate them: "Because you do not belong to the world, . . . therefore the world hates you" (John 15:19 NRSV; cf. also John 17:14–19). Today, unfortunately, many people despise Christians, not for their unswerving obedience to Christ, but because of the hypocritical disconnect between Jesus's teaching and our actions. But precisely because Jesus expected his followers to live so differently from their neighbors, he could say that they would also be salt and light, preserving and even changing a corrupt, immoral world (Matt. 5:13–14).

Jesus was ruthless with the materialists of his day who loved their money more than God. One day a wealthy, prominent citizen approached Jesus, asking what he must do to inherit eternal life. Their conversation soon revealed a devout person who faithfully kept the commandments. But Jesus knew that this rich man loved his money too much. So Jesus ordered him to sell all, give his wealth to the poor, and follow Jesus. As the wealthy materialist sadly turned away, Jesus said, "It is easier for a camel to go through the eye of a needle than for someone who is rich to enter the kingdom of God" (Luke 18:25 NRSV). Jesus urged his followers to imitate the lilies of the field, to trust in God rather than worry about the material things they need (Luke 12:22). Rather than worry about food and clothing, Jesus said, "Seek first his kingdom and his righteousness, and all these things will be given to you as well" (Matt. 6:33).

Jesus denounced lukewarm folk who wanted both to worship God and practice sin. "No servant can serve two masters. Either he will hate the one and love the other, or he will be devoted to the one and despise the other. You cannot serve both God and Money" (Luke 16:13). What was the Pharisees' response? They sneered! Like many contemporary Christians, they "loved money" (v. 14).

Unlike many Christians today who justify easy divorce, Jesus sharply restricted the grounds for divorce. In Jesus's day, it was easy for a man to divorce his wife for almost any reason. Jesus said no! "Anyone who divorces his wife, except for marital unfaithfulness, and marries another woman commits adultery" (Matt. 19:9).

Jesus insisted that anyone who loves him "will obey my teaching" (John 14:23). But not in our own strength. It is only as we abide in Christ who is the vine that we branches can obey Christ and bear fruit. "Those who abide in me and I in them bear much fruit, because apart from me you can do nothing" (John 15:5 NRSV). How do we abide in Christ? Not just by believing in him, but also by obeying him! "If you keep my commandments, you will abide in my love, just as I have kept my Father's commandments and abide in his love" (v. 10).

Again, we dare never suppose that we can keep Christ's commands in our own strength. All who receive Christ are "born of God" and become children of God (John 1:13). As Jesus told Nicodemus, "no one can see the kingdom of God without being born from above [or born anew]" (John 3:3 NRSV). To those who do trust and obey him, Jesus promises, he and the Father "will come to them and make [their] home with them" (14:23 NRSV).

Knowing that his disciples would enjoy the very presence of the living God at the center of their lives, Jesus knew it was realistic to give them the radical command, "Just as I have loved you, you also should love one another" (John 13:34 NRSV). In fact, Jesus prayed to the Father, surely expecting his prayer to be answered, that his followers would care for each other with such loving unity "that the world may believe that you have sent me" (John 17:21).

Jesus gladly forgave even the most vile of sinners. But he called them to costly discipleship and holy obedience, promising that he himself would provide the strength as he came to live in them.

Acts

The picture of the first Christians in Jerusalem presented in the early chapters of Acts is one of astonishing love and joyous fellowship. Dramatic economic sharing was the norm: "All who believed were together and had all things in common; they would sell their possessions and goods and distribute the proceeds to all, as any had need" (Acts 2:44–45 NRSV). From later sections of Acts, it becomes clear that families retained private property. Membership in the new fellowship did not mean one must place all property in a common purse. But the economic sharing was so extensive that observers were compelled to say that "there were no needy persons among them" (4:34). This astonishing economic sharing produced powerful evangelistic results! After saying that these Jerusalem Christians "shared everything they had," Luke adds, "With great power the apostles continued to testify to the resurrection of the Lord Jesus" (4:32–33).

These early Christians certainly were not perfect. Acts 6 describes how the Hebrew leadership neglected widows from the Greek-speaking minority. So what did they do? They appointed seven deacons (their Greek names indicate they are all from the Greek-speaking minority!) to take charge of the care of all the widows. What was the result of this prompt correction of racial and economic discrimination? The last verse of the story says, "So the word of God spread. The number of disciples in Jerusalem increased rapidly" (Acts 6:7). Again, integrity and obedience in the body of Christ have powerful evangelistic results.

Romans

Paul begins his letter to the Romans (Paul's most systematic theological statement) with a wonderful exposition of justification by faith alone. Everyone, both Jew and Gentile, is a sinner. Nobody can stand before our holy God on the basis of his or her good deeds. But thank God, we do not have to try; all we need to do is have faith in Christ. "For we hold," Paul writes, "that a person is justified by faith apart from works" (3:28 NRSV). Abraham believed God, and Abraham's faith was reckoned as righteousness (4:3). So too the psalmist who declared that when God forgives our iniquities, he no longer reckons our sins to us (4:6–8). Justification—right standing before the most holy Being in the universe—is truly by faith alone, not good works.

Quickly, however, Paul squelches an objection to this powerful teaching of justification by grace through faith. Should believers go on sinning so that God can continue demonstrating his astonishing mercy? The very idea horrifies Paul: "By no means!" (6:2). Why not? Because Christians have actually *died* to sin. In baptism, we die with Christ. Our old sinful self is crucified with Christ. Furthermore, just as Christ was raised from death, so we are raised to a new life in Christ. Therefore, Paul concludes, we dare not let sin reign in our mortal bodies.

Listen to this whole amazing argument of St. Paul:

> What shall we say, then? Shall we go on sinning so that grace may increase? By no means! We died to sin; how can we live in it any longer? Or don't you know that all of us who were baptized into Christ Jesus were baptized into his death? We were therefore buried with him through baptism into death in order that, just as Christ was raised from the dead through the glory of the Father, we too may live a new life.
>
> If we have been united with him like this in his death, we will certainly also be united with him in his resurrection. For we know that our old self was crucified with him so that the body of sin might be done away with, that we should no longer be slaves to sin—because anyone who has died has been freed from sin.
>
> Now if we died with Christ, we believe that we will also live with him. For we know that since Christ was raised from the dead, he cannot die again; death no longer has mastery over him. The death he died, he died to sin once for all; but the life he lives, he lives to God.
>
> In the same way, count yourselves dead to sin but alive to God in Christ Jesus. Therefore do not let sin reign in your mortal body so that you obey its evil desires. Do not offer the parts of your body to sin, as instruments of wickedness, but rather offer yourselves to God, as those who have been brought from death to life; and offer the parts of your body to him as instruments of righteousness. For sin shall not be your master, because you are not under law, but under grace.

What then? Shall we sin because we are not under law but under grace? By no means! . . . You have been set free from sin and have become slaves to righteousness.

Romans 6:1–15, 18

Paul is adamant. Formerly, we were slaves to sin. And the benefit we received was death, finally, eternal death. "But now that you have been set free from sin and have become slaves to God," the benefit is holiness and the gift of eternal life (6:19–23).

Nor is Paul finished describing the amazing moral and ethical transformation that comes with genuine faith in Christ. In chapter 7, Paul vividly wrestles with the power of sin. He describes the way the teaching of the law provoked sinful persons to rebel and sin still more. In stark terms, Paul also describes the way he—and all of us—are torn between an inner desire to obey God and a conflicting desire to please self. But his conclusion is not despair or resignation but assurance that Christ rescues us from this wrenching conflict:

Through Christ Jesus the law of the Spirit of life set me free from the law of sin and death. For what the law was powerless to do in that it was weakened by the sinful nature, God did by sending his own Son . . . *in order that the righteous requirements of the law might be fully met in us*, who do not live according to the sinful nature, but according to the Spirit.

Romans 8:2–4, italics mine

Because the Holy Spirit dwells in believers' hearts, empowering them and transforming their character, Paul says they can now live the way God intends.

Christians, Paul insists, are not controlled by their old sinful nature, but by the Spirit. "But if Christ is in you, your body is dead because of sin, yet your spirit is alive because of righteousness" (8:10). Therefore, we have an *obligation*, Paul argues, to put to death the deeds of the old sinful nature (vv. 12–13).

At the beginning of chapter 12, Paul switches from careful theological argument to ethical instruction with an amazing passage. First he urges Christians to offer our "bodies as living sacrifices" to God (v. 1)—to surrender ourselves totally and unconditionally to God. Then follow the amazing words of verse 2: "Do not conform any longer to the pattern of this world, but be transformed by the renewing of your mind." Or as J. B. Phillips put it so well, "Don't let the world squeeze you into its mold." Paul expects Christians to be radically countercultural people living according to Jesus rather than the world.

In the rest of the letter, Paul mentions things that conformity to Christ means: giving generously to those in need (12:8); sincere love for brothers and sisters (vv. 9–10); blessing those who persecute you (v. 14); sharing others' joys and sorrows (v. 15); not repaying evil for evil (v. 17); keeping the commandments which are summed up in Jesus's rule to "love your neighbor as yourself" (13:9); and putting aside drunkenness, sexual immorality, and jealousy (13:13). Paul sums it all up with the command: "Clothe yourselves with the Lord Jesus Christ and do not think about how to gratify the desires of the sinful nature" (13:14).

What an incredible picture of the way that faith in Christ transforms and sanctifies broken sinners. If Paul is even close to being right about what it means to be a Christian, one can only weep at the scandalous behavior of Christians today.

First and Second Corinthians

These two letters remind us not to romanticize the early church. They witness to the realities of quarreling, jealousy, angry lawsuits between Christians, and sexual immorality within the church. Paul's response, however, is not to lower the standards to accommodate their failures, but rather to demand repentance and holy living. So a church member is committing gross sexual misconduct (1 Cor. 5)? Put the man out of the church! Indeed, Paul adds a long list of sins that require church discipline, ordering the Corinthian Christians "not to associate with anyone who bears the name of brother or sister who is sexually immoral, or greedy, or is an idolater, reviler, drunkard, or robber" (1 Cor. 5:11 NRSV). So Christians are suing each other in secular courts? Shame on them! They should resolve their disputes with the help of other brothers and sisters in the body of Christ and even prefer losing property to suing another Christian in a secular court (1 Cor. 6:1–7).

Then Paul adds a powerful, general warning:

Do you not know that the wicked will not inherit the kingdom of God? Do not be deceived: Neither the sexually immoral nor idolaters nor adulterers nor male prostitutes nor homosexual offenders nor thieves nor the greedy nor drunkards nor slanderers nor swindlers will inherit the kingdom of God.

1 Corinthians 6:9–10

How many preachers today speak that clearly about the sins of greed, adultery, and slander?

Paul urges the Corinthians to purify themselves "from everything that contaminates body and spirit, perfecting holiness out of reverence for God" (2 Cor. 7:1). He also devotes two entire chapters (8–9) of his second letter to a long plea for the Corinthian church to give a generous offering for the poor Christians in Jerusalem.

The last verse of 2 Corinthians 3 is one of the most powerful statements about the sanctification that Paul expects of Christians and knows is possible in Christ: "And all of us, with unveiled faces, seeing the glory of the Lord as though reflected in a mirror, are being transformed into the same image from one degree of glory to another" (NRSV). Genuine Christians look directly into the face of Christ. The result? We are transformed into the very likeness of Christ! Not all at once, to be sure. The present tense—we *are being transformed*—indicates an ongoing process of sanctification. Day by day we are slowly becoming more and more like him. We do not expect absolute perfection now. But there is no room whatsoever in this verse for Christians to continue year after year in the same sin, repeating a ritual confession every week and making no progress in holiness. Year by year, genuine Christians are transformed more and more into the very character of Christ.

Galatians

The center of Galatians is its ringing rejection of justification by works. But Paul does not forget about sanctification: "Those who belong to Christ Jesus have crucified the sinful nature with its passion and desires" (5:24). We live by the Spirit and therefore can display the fruits of the Spirit: love, joy, peace, patience, kindness, goodness, faithfulness, and self-control (5:22–23). As in 2 Corinthians, Paul lists a number of sinful acts and bluntly warns that those who do such things will not be saved. "The acts of the sinful nature," writes Paul, "are obvious: sexual immorality, impurity and debauchery; idolatry and witchcraft; hatred, discord, jealousy, fits of rage, selfish ambition, dissensions, factions and envy; drunkenness, orgies, and the like. I warn you, as I did before, that those who live like this will not inherit the kingdom of God" (5:19–21).

Paul knows that Christians are not perfect. He gives instructions for restoring a brother or sister who is "caught in a sin" (6:1). Others should prayerfully, gently restore the erring person. But Paul feels compelled to warn that "God cannot be mocked, for you reap whatever you sow. If you sow to your own flesh, you will reap corruption from the flesh; but if you sow to the Spirit, you will reap eternal life from the Spirit" (6:7–8 NRSV). How can contemporary "Christians" who behave just like their unbelieving neighbors read such a passage without fear and trembling?

Ephesians

In Ephesians Paul again combines salvation by grace alone with obedient Christian living. We are saved "by grace through faith" as God's sheer gift so no one can boast (2:8–9). Then in the very next sentence, Paul adds, "For we are God's workmanship, created in Christ Jesus *to do good works*" (italics mine).

Ephesians 4 contains one of Paul's most powerful, extended statements about the radical ethical transformation that genuine Christian faith produces. Paul begins by urging the Ephesian Christians to "live a life worthy of the calling you have received" (v. 1). That means humility, gentleness, patience, and love. The purpose of the various spiritual gifts given to different persons is to build up the body of Christ so that we all reach "the whole measure of the fullness of Christ" (v. 13). What a standard!

On the very authority of the Lord, Paul insists that they "must no longer live as the Gentiles" who "indulge in every kind of impurity, with a continual lust for more" (vv. 17–19). Paul reminds them that they had been taught a better way: "You were taught, with regard to your former way of life, to put off your old self, which is being corrupted by its deceitful desires; to be made new in the attitude of your minds; and to put on the new self, created to be like God in true righteousness and holiness" (vv. 22–24). Our very nature has been renewed by Christ.

44

Paul then proceeds to list many things that Spirit-filled Christians should avoid: unwholesome talk, bitterness, rage, anger, slander. Instead, we must be kind and compassionate to each other (vv. 29–30). Indeed, Christians must imitate God himself and Christ on the cross. We are to forgive "each other, just as in Christ God forgave you. *Be imitators of God,* therefore, as dearly loved children, and live a life of love, just as Christ loved us and gave himself up for us as a fragrant offering and sacrifice to God" (4:32–5:2, italics mine).

In the next sentence, Paul adds to the list of sinful activities of which "there must not be even a hint" among Christians (5:3): sexual immorality, greed, obscenity, coarse joking. And still one more time, Paul declares that such sinners go to hell! "No immoral, impure or greedy person—such a man is an idolater—has any inheritance in the kingdom of Christ and of God" (5:5). Because of such things, God's wrath falls on "those who are disobedient" (5:6). One wonders what language Paul would use if he were speaking to the substantial number of evangelicals today who claim that adulterous sex is morally acceptable.

Formerly, we lived in darkness. But now in Christ, we can and must live as children of the light—having "nothing to do with the fruitless deeds of darkness" (5:11). "Be careful then how you live," Paul concludes (5:15).

Where are contemporary preachers warning us, as clearly as St. Paul did, about the terrible evil and awful consequences of unholy lifestyles? One wonders how many materialistic Americans are guilty of greed, which Paul explicitly says is idolatry (5:5). How many preachers remind their materialistic members that they are worshiping an idol and have no place in the kingdom of God?

Philippians and Colossians

In Philippians the references to sanctification are brief but clear. Paul prays that the recipients may be "pure and blameless," filled with "the fruit of righteousness that comes through Jesus Christ" (1:10–11). Reminding them that they are "united with Christ," Paul urges them to show humility and mutual love. Christ himself in his self-sacrificing incarnation and cross is the model to imitate (2:1–11). Do everything, Paul urges the Philippians, "so that you may become blameless and pure, children of God without fault in a crooked and depraved generation" (2:14–15).

Colossians 3 contains another stunning statement of how and why Christians live radically transformed lives. "For you have died, and your life is now hidden with Christ in God" (v. 3). Paul is using the same theology of baptism that he articulated in Romans 6. We died to our sinful selves and "have been raised with Christ" (v. 1). What is the proper response of baptized believers? Paul commands us to put to death the old self of sin and put on the new self patterned after Christ: "Put to death, therefore, whatever belongs to your earthly nature" (v. 5). Then he promptly offers his usual list of sins, including greed, which he again labels idolatry. Formerly, they walked in such evil ways, but "now you must rid yourselves of all such things" (v. 8). How is this possible? "You have taken off your old self with its practices and have put on the new self, which is being renewed in knowledge in the image of its Creator" (vv. 9–10). Again, the present tense reminds us that this ethical renewal is an ongoing process.

In the next verse, Paul draws the obvious conclusion for racial, ethnic, and class prejudice and discrimination: "Here [i.e., where we have died to sin and arisen with Christ] there is no Greek or Jew, circumcised or uncircumcised, barbarian, Scythian, slave or free, but Christ is all, and is in all" (v. 11). With biblical teaching like that, how can it be that evangelicals are the most racially prejudiced people in our country?

Pastoral Letters and Hebrews

Again, the references are brief but powerful. God has saved us and called us to "a holy life" (2 Tim. 1:9). According to Titus 2:13–14, part of the very purpose of Christ's redeeming work was to "redeem us from all wickedness" and purify a group of people "eager to do what is good."

Hebrews 10 contains a terrible warning to Christians who continue to sin: "If we deliberately keep on sinning after we have received the knowledge of the truth, no sacrifice for sins is left, but only a fearful expectation of judgment and of raging fire that will consume the enemies of God" (10:26–27). Christians who persist in sin trample the Son of God underfoot and insult the Holy Spirit: "It is a dreadful thing to fall into the hands of the living God" (v. 31).

The Letters of James and Peter

James demands actions, not just words: "Faith by itself, if it is not accompanied by action, is dead" (2:17). James is talking about supposed Christians who see brothers and sisters who need food and clothing and do nothing. He writes, "Religion that God our Father accepts as pure and faultless is this: to look after orphans and widows in their distress and to keep oneself from being polluted by the world" (1:27).

Peter knows that Christians have experienced new birth: "you have been born again" through the word of God (1 Peter 1:4, 23). He puts it even more strongly in his second letter. We have divine "power" to live a godly life; indeed, we "participate in the *divine nature* and escape the corruption in the world caused by evil desires" (1:3–4). His conclusion? "For this very reason, make every effort to add to your faith goodness" (v. 5).

We must not be conformed to the evil desires of our old life, but live as obedient children. "Just as he who called you is holy," Peter urges, "so be holy in all you do; for it is written, 'Be holy, because I am holy'" (1 Peter 1:14–15). Peter notes that the pagans "think it strange" that their Christian neighbors no longer join them in debauchery, lust, drunkenness, and idolatry (1 Peter 4:3–4). Apparently, the countercultural lifestyle of these early Christians was obvious to outsiders. Eventually, Peter believed, these pagan neighbors would glorify God for the moral integrity of the Christians they observed (1 Peter 2:11–12).

First John

Perhaps no other New Testament writing so intricately weaves together orthodoxy and orthopraxis—right theology and right action. Anyone who denies that Jesus is God in the flesh is a heretic, and anyone who claims to love God but refuses to love brother or sister does not know God (2:22–23; 3:17).

What is the purpose of the letter John writes to his "little children" in Christ? The answer is simple: "So that you will not sin" (2:1).

He bluntly insists that genuine Christians do not continue to sin. Everyone who accepts Christ is born of God and "no one who is born of God will continue to sin, because God's seed remains in him; he cannot go on sinning, because he has been born of God" (3:9). And again, "No one who lives in him keeps on sinning. No one who continues to sin has either seen him or known him" (3:6). Equally pointed is John's earlier declaration: "If we claim to have fellowship with him [Christ], yet walk in the darkness, we lie" (1:6).

At the same time, John is equally clear that Christians are not perfect: "If we claim to be without sin, we deceive ourselves and the truth is not in us" (1:8; cf. v. 10). If we see a brother or sister committing a sin, we should pray for them so that their sin does not lead to death (5:16–17). Our proper response to sin is confession. God, in turn, forgives *and* purifies. Few biblical texts are more wonderful than this promise: "If we confess our sins, he is faithful and just and will forgive us our sins *and purify us from all unrighteousness*" (1:9, italics mine). God does more than reckon forgiveness to us. God purifies us, cleansing us from sin.

Therefore, John insists, we can tell who is a Christian by observing their actions:

> Now by this we may be sure that we know him, if we
> obey his commandments. Whoever says, "I have come

to know him," but does not obey his commandments, is a liar, and in such a person the truth does not exist; but whoever obeys his word, truly in this person the love of God has reached perfection. By this we may be sure that we are in him: whoever says, "I abide in him," ought to walk just as he walked.

2:3–6 NRSV

Later, he writes, "This is how we know who the children of God are and who the children of the devil are: Anyone who does not do what is right is not a child of God; nor is anyone who does not love his brother" (3:10).

Not surprisingly, John insists that genuine Christians love others in practical ways. If we see a brother or sister in material need and do not help, God's love is not in us (3:17). Since Christ is our model, we must "not love with words or tongue but with actions and in truth" (3:18). Love of God, love of others, and obedience to God are inseparably intertwined: "This is how we know that we love the children of God: by loving God and carrying out his command" (5:2).

I don't know if John would be more puzzled or angry at the scandalous behavior of today's evangelical Christians. Probably he would just weep. We proudly trumpet our orthodox doctrine of Christ as true God and true man and then disobey his teaching. We divorce, though doing so is contrary to his commands. We are the richest people in human history and know that tens of millions of brothers and sisters in Christ live in grinding poverty, and we give only a pittance, and almost all of that goes to our local congregation. Only a tiny fraction of what we do give ever reaches poor Christians in other places. Christ died to create one new multicultural body of believers, yet we display more racism than liberal Christians who doubt his deity.

Our evangelistic efforts are often crippled by our behavior. In both Acts 2 and 6, it is clear that the loving, obedient actions of the first Christians attracted people to Christ.

The same was true during the early centuries of the Christian faith. Numerous documents from those years demonstrate that Christians' behavior was unusual. Writing in the middle of the second century, Justin Martyr said of Christians:

> Those who once delighted in fornication now embrace chastity alone; . . . we who once took most pleasure in accumulating wealth and property now . . . share with everyone in need; we who hated and killed one another and would not associate with men of different tribes because of their different customs now, since the coming of Christ, live familiarly with them and pray for our enemies.[1]

Writing in about AD 125, the Christian apologist Aristides described Christians with these words:

> They walk in all humility and kindness, and falsehood is not found among them, and they love one another. They despise not the widow, and grieve not the orphan. He that hath, distributeth liberally to him that hath not. If they see a stranger, they bring him under their roof, and rejoice over him, as it were their own brother: for they call themselves brethren, not after the flesh, but after the spirit and God; but

when one of their poor passes away from the world, and any
of them see him, then he provides for his burial according
to his ability; and if they hear that any of their number is
imprisoned or oppressed for the name of their Messiah, all
of them provide for his needs; and if it is possible that he
may be delivered, they deliver him. And if there is among
them a man that is poor and needy, and they have not an
abundance of necessaries, they fast two or three days that
they may supply the needy with their necessary food.[2]

In both of these documents, the early Christians' economic
sharing and concern for the poor are especially striking.
By AD 250, the church at Rome supported fifteen hundred
needy persons.[3] Outsiders were amazed by the love that they
saw in the Christian community. Tertullian (AD 155–220)
reported that even the enemies of Christianity considered
the mutual love of Christians to be their "distinctive sign":
"Our care for the derelict and our active love have become
our distinctive sign before the enemy. . . . See, they say, how
they love one another and how ready they are to die for
each other."[4]

Perhaps the most striking commentary on the countercultural character of Christian behavior comes from a
grudging comment by a pagan emperor. During his short
reign (AD 361–63), Julian the Apostate tried to roll back
several decades of toleration and stamp out Christianity.
But he was forced to admit to a fellow pagan that "the
godless Galileans [Christians] feed not only their poor
but ours also." With chagrin, he acknowledged that his
fellow pagans did not even help each other: "Those who
belong to us look in vain for the help that we should ren-
der them."[5]

We have seen the stunning contrast between what Jesus and the early church said and did and what so many evangelicals do today. Hopefully that contrast will drive us to our knees, first to repent and then to ask God to help us understand the causes of this scandalous failure and the steps we can take to correct it.

Cheap Grace vs.
the Whole Gospel

All the evangelism in the world from a church that is not herself holy and righteous will not be worth a hill of beans in world-changing power.

Peter E. Gillquist

So why this scandal? And what can we do about it?
We must do more than cringe and cry at the huge gap between biblical vision and contemporary evangelical practice. We must beg God to show us what to do to make things better. In this and the next chapter, I wrestle with some hard questions: What caused this tragedy? And what can we do to end the scandal and nurture a more faithful church?

Close to the center of the problem is a cluster of unbiblical ideas and practices that amount to what Dietrich

Bonhoeffer called "cheap grace." Cheap grace results when we reduce the gospel to forgiveness of sins; limit salvation to personal fire insurance against hell; misunderstand persons as primarily souls; at best, grasp only half of what the Bible says about sin; embrace the individualism, materialism, and relativism of our current culture; lack a biblical understanding and practice of the church; and fail to teach a biblical worldview. We must probe these problems and explore how to understand and live the much richer, fuller, biblical teaching on the gospel, salvation, persons, sin, and the church. That, of course, means wholeheartedly embracing biblical revelation as God's fully inspired, fully authoritative truth.

Many recent evangelical authors have deplored the way cheap grace has wormed its way into the evangelical world. In a recent cover story in *Christianity Today*, George Barna decries our "costless faith," concluding that we have made it too easy to be "born again."[1] Slick evangelical marketers have offered eternal salvation as a free gift if you just say yes to a simple formula: " 'God loves you, humankind blew the relationship, but He has a plan for your life; just saying the magic words triggers the contract' was what we told people." The response? "Boomers studied the offer and realized it was a no-lose proposition: eternal security at nothing down, no future payments, just simple verbal assent. The deal specified nothing about life change."[2] Why not accept a no-cost fire insurance policy? The result, Barna sadly notes, is "born-again" people living just like everybody else.

In *Why We Haven't Changed the World*, Peter E. Gillquist reflected upon his years and years of passionate evangelism as a leader with a large, prominent evangelical organization. Eagerly, persistently, fervently, he talked to thousands of people, inviting them to Christ. By the early eighties, he concluded, evangelistic activity was perhaps more prominent than any time "in the whole *history* of the church."[3]

Slowly, however, Gillquist realized that the world was not changing. Why? Because the church itself had lost its holiness and righteousness. He writes, "All the evangelism in the world from a church that is not herself holy and righteous will not be worth a hill of beans in world-changing power."[4] Modern evangelicalism, he concludes, is in a "modern Babylonian captivity and we do not yet know it."[5]

John G. Stackhouse Jr., professor of theology at Regent College and frequent writer for *Christianity Today*, laments evangelicals' "perpetual adolescence." Many evangelicals, he says, lie, cheat, and otherwise sin against others in "already-forgiven bliss" with an attitude of "I'm-cool-'cause-Jesus-loves-me-and-so-I-don't-owe-you-a-thing."[6]

The Gospel and Salvation

I am convinced that at the heart of our problem is a one-sided, unbiblical, reductionist understanding of the gospel and salvation. Too many evangelicals in too many ways give the impression that the really important part of the gospel is forgiveness of sins. If we just repeat the formula and say we want Jesus to forgive our sins, we are Christians. Notice, however, how this can so easily lead to cheap grace. If all there is to accepting the gospel is receiving the forgiveness of sins, one can accept the gospel, become a Christian, and then go on living the same adulterous, materialistic, racist life that one lived before. Salvation becomes, not a life-transforming experience that reorients every corner of life, but a one-way ticket to heaven, and one can live like hell until one gets there.

I believe with all my heart there is no way for sinful persons to earn God's acceptance. Thank God that the holy Creator is the merciful Redeemer who promises to forgive our sins if we repent and trust in Christ's atoning death for us. We *are* justified by faith alone. As we shall see in a moment, however, the New Testament does not stop there. We cannot accept Christ as Savior without embracing him as Lord. A genuine personal relationship with Christ brings sweeping transformation of our sinful selves. In the New Testament the gospel and salvation involve far more than forgiveness of sins.

Unfortunately, even our best theologians sometimes overstate the wonderful doctrine of forgiveness of sins. One can understand how Martin Luther, in his important struggle to free the gospel from works righteousness, could say that justification by faith is "the principal article of Christian doctrine."[7] Tragically, such a statement taken by itself easily leads to a neglect of sanctification and holy, obedient living. Today our most outstanding evangelical theologians sometimes say things like the following: "Justification by faith appears to us, as it does to all evangelicals, to be the heart and hub, the paradigm and essence, of the whole economy of God's saving grace. Like Atlas, it bears a world on its shoulders, the entire evangelical knowledge of God's love in Christ toward sinners."[8] Fortunately, in many other places, the same authors make it very clear that they believe sanctification is important.

There is simply no biblical justification for saying that the glorious truth of justification by faith alone is more important than the astonishing reality that the Risen Lord now lives in his disciples, transforming them day by day into his very likeness. Justification and sanctification are *both* central parts of the biblical teaching on the gospel and salvation. To overstate the importance of the one is to run the danger of neglecting the other. And that is certainly what popular evangelicalism has done. Whether emphasizing simplistic slogans such as "once-in-grace-always-in-grace" or focusing on seeker-friendly strategies that neglect costly discipleship, we have propagated the heretical notion that people can receive forgiveness without sanctification, heaven without holiness. Notions of cheap grace are at the core of today's scandalous evangelical disobedience.

The Gospel

One of the most astonishing ironies of contemporary evangelicalism is that most evangelicals do not even define the gospel the way Jesus did! One would think that the part of the Christian community that most prides itself on faithfulness to the Scriptures and on an orthodox doctrine of Christ would consider it important to define the gospel the way Jesus did. But that is simply not the case.

Jesus did not define the gospel as the forgiveness of sins, although again and again he offered free, unmerited forgiveness. The vast majority of New Testament scholars today, whether evangelical or liberal, agree that the central aspect of Jesus's teaching was the gospel of the kingdom of God. The words "kingdom of God" or Matthew's equivalent, "kingdom of heaven," appear 122 times in Matthew, Mark, and Luke, and 92 times they are on the lips of Jesus himself.

Both Matthew and Mark explicitly summarize Jesus's gospel as the "good news of the kingdom." Twice, Matthew uses almost identical words to summarize Jesus's activity: "Jesus went throughout Galilee, teaching in their synagogues, preaching the *good news of the kingdom*, and healing every disease and sickness among the people" (Matt. 4:23; 9:35, italics mine). At the beginning of his account of Jesus's public ministry, Mark summarizes his understanding of the content of Jesus's gospel: "After John was put in prison, Jesus went into Galilee, proclaiming the good news of God. 'The time has come,' he said. '*The kingdom of God is near*. Repent and believe the good news'" (Mark 1:14–15, italics mine). Clearly, Mark understood the core of Jesus's gospel to be the gospel of the kingdom.

Matthew and Mark were simply following Jesus's own self-understanding. Jesus defined his mission explicitly in terms of preaching the gospel of the kingdom: "I must preach the good news of the kingdom to the other towns also, *because that is why I was sent*" (Luke 4:43, italics mine). And when Jesus sent out the twelve and later the seventy-two on mission trips, he told them that the content of their preaching should be precisely the kingdom of God: "As you go," he told the twelve, "preach this message: 'The kingdom of heaven is near.' Heal the sick, raise the dead, cleanse those who have leprosy" (Matt. 10:7–8). "When you enter a town," he instructed the seventy-two as he commissioned them, "heal the sick who are there and tell them, 'The kingdom of God is near you'" (Luke 10:8–9). There can be no doubt that Jesus's gospel was the good news of the kingdom.

But what do the words mean? What was Jesus saying? Long before, the prophets had promised that someday God would send the Messiah who would bring a new right relationship with God and neighbor.[9] God would forgive his people's sins in a new way and bring peace and justice. Jesus came proclaiming, first carefully and then more and more openly, that he was the long-expected Messiah and that the messianic kingdom of God which the Messiah was to usher in was actually dawning in his own person and work. When the Pharisees attributed Jesus's ability to cast out demons to Satan, Jesus retorted, "If I drive out demons by the Spirit of God, then the kingdom of God *has come* upon you" (Matt. 12:28, italics mine). He uses the past tense! The messianic kingdom has already begun to arrive, though it does not come in its fullness, of course, until Jesus's second coming.

In parable after parable about God's astonishing love for sinners, Jesus clearly taught that the only way to enter this dawning kingdom was by sheer grace. The Pharisees of Jesus's day claimed that the messianic kingdom would come if all the Jews obeyed the law perfectly. The violent Jewish revolutionaries thought the Messiah would come if everyone took up arms. Jesus said no, the only way to enter the kingdom is by accepting God's freely given mercy. Forgiveness of sins is at the center of Jesus's proclamation of the gospel of the kingdom.

But it is only part of it. Jesus did not go around the country whispering to isolated hermits, "Your sins are forgiven." Jesus gathered together a circle of disciples. He formed a new community of forgiven sinners—tax collectors, prostitutes, fishermen—who began to live according to Jesus's kingdom values and challenge the status quo where it was wrong. He challenged the rich to share with the poor in costly ways (Luke 6:34–35; Matt. 25:31–46). He rejected the way society marginalized and neglected lepers, disabled folk, and women. He condemned political leaders for the way they preferred domination to servanthood (Mark 10:42–45). And he rejected the popular, violent Jewish revolutionaries of his time who were calling for armed rebellion against Rome. Love your enemies, he commanded (Matt. 5:44).

Jesus's gospel of the kingdom included both vertical and horizontal aspects. Yes, one enters this kingdom by sheer grace because God gladly forgives prodigal sons and daughters who repent. That is the vertical part. But equally central to Jesus's words and actions was the new horizontal community of disciples, forgiven sinners all, who began to imitate Jesus in living according to the norms of the dawning kingdom—a kingdom where the poor would receive justice, and peace would prevail. Jesus and his followers healed the sick, cared for the poor, and welcomed the marginalized into their fellowship. That is why Paul says in Ephesians 2–3 that the very existence of a new multiethnic body of believers, where hostile groups of Jews and Gentiles are becoming harmoniously united, is part of the gospel. This is the mystery—the gospel—that Paul preaches: "This mystery is that through the gospel the

Gentiles are heirs together with Israel, members together of one body" (Eph. 3:6).

How did Jesus announce his gospel? By word *and* deed! Words would have been enough if his gospel was just the forgiveness of sins. But since his gospel included the wonderful fact that the long-expected messianic kingdom was now actually becoming visible in history, Jesus had to demonstrate the presence of this kingdom, not just talk about it. That's why the writers of the Gospels regularly say that Jesus preached and healed. Jesus's dawning kingdom brought healing to body and soul. You could see and touch this arriving kingdom.

When Christians today reduce the gospel to forgiveness of sins, they are offering a one-sided, heretical message that is flatly unfaithful to the Jesus they worship as Lord and God. Only if we recover Jesus's gospel of the kingdom and allow its power to so transform our sinful selves that our Christian congregations (always imperfect to be sure) become visible holy signs of the dawning kingdom will we be faithful to Jesus. Only then will our evangelistic words recover integrity and power.

Fortunately, a recent evangelical consensus declaration on the gospel is much better than other evangelical statements. The new declaration insists, "The Gospel requires of all believers . . . submission to all that [God] has revealed in his written word." The declaration argues that saving faith includes both justification by faith alone and sanctification by the power of the Spirit. "We affirm that saving faith results in sanctification, the transformation of life in conformity to Christ. . . . We deny that saving faith includes only mental acceptance of the Gospel." The statement continues,

"Genuine faith acknowledges and depends upon Jesus as Lord and shows itself in growing obedience to the divine commands."[10] These important declarations naturally follow a right understanding of Jesus's gospel of the kingdom of God.

Salvation

The same one-sided, reductionist misunderstanding that has distorted our conception of the gospel has led us away from a full-fledged biblical understanding of salvation. For too many evangelicals, Jesus's work of salvation is reduced to the cross, and the cross is reduced to substitutionary atonement. Salvation thus becomes nothing more than saying the right words so my sins are forgiven and I can avoid hell.

This understanding is an important part of biblical salvation. We all deserve divine punishment. Thank God that our holy, awesomely righteous Judge gladly forgives our sins as we trust in Christ's death for us. Thank God that throughout our lives, devout Christians, knowing their continuing imperfection, can cling to the cross as the only basis for God's acceptance of us. Thank God for books like Philip Yancey's *What's So Amazing about Grace?* that remind us of the wonder and power of forgiveness.[11]

Thank God, too, that there is so much more to a biblical understanding of salvation. Christ not only forgives us, he also changes us. And he transforms not just our inner selves but our external behavior. Christ calls us to accept him as Lord as well as Savior. He calls us to conversion—a fundamental reversal of direction—and a life of costly discipleship.

In the power of the Holy Spirit, God creates a new social order, a new community of believers, where all relationships are being restored to holiness. All of this is part of what the New Testament means by salvation.

In chapter 2 we saw the sweeping way St. Paul claims that genuine Christians die to their old selves and rise to a new life in Christ. Each believer's whole being is being changed, day by day, more and more into the very likeness of Christ.

These transformed believers act differently in all their social relationships. Acts 2 and 4 describe the stunning economic sharing that occurred among the first Christians. Social and economic relationships in the body of Christ were so radically different from those of the rest of the world that Paul boasted credibly that the church was a place of neither Jew nor Greek, male nor female, slave nor free. All this is part of what the New Testament also means by salvation.

The story of Zacchaeus contains vivid evidence that for Jesus and the New Testament, salvation includes new social, economic behavior among those who embrace Jesus. Luke 19 tells a striking story about a wicked tax collector named Zacchaeus. He had gladly piled up riches through the unjust economic tax system in which the Roman conquerors allowed local "subcontractors" to collect far more taxes than they passed on to Rome. But when Zacchaeus met Jesus, he was changed—dramatically. He repaid fourfold all whom he had cheated. Then he gave half of his goods to the poor. The story ends with Jesus's words, "Today *salvation* has come to this house" (19:9).

There is not a single word in the entire passage about the forgiveness of sins. Now I am sure Jesus did forgive the rascal. Zacchaeus surely needed it! But what the text addresses is the dramatically transformed economic behavior and relationships that Zacchaeus exhibits after he comes face-to-face with Jesus. That, too, Jesus says explicitly, is part of what biblical salvation means.

Some evangelicals give the impression that the only reason the Son of God came to earth was to die. This, of course, was one reason he came to earth, but it was far from the only reason. He also lived among us to teach and model a godly life to show us how the Creator wants us to live. Furthermore, he came to burst from the tomb and conquer the power of death.

There is also an evangelical tendency to think the only purpose of Jesus's death was to offer a sacrifice for our sins. The New Testament explanation of the meaning of the cross does include the wonderful truth that Christ took our place on the cross, but there is much more to it than that! First John 3:16 says explicitly that we learn what real love is like through Jesus's model on the cross. And 1 John 3:8 declares that "the reason the Son of God appeared was to destroy the devil's work" (also Heb. 2:14–15). As I argue in much more detail elsewhere, the moral, the substitutionary, and the *Christus victor* (Christ conquering the power of sin and Satan) views of the atonement are all part of the wonderfully complex New Testament understanding of the cross.[12] All that is part of salvation.

Also central to what the New Testament tells us about salvation is the fact that Christ is both Savior and Lord. In fact, the New Testament uses "Savior" for Jesus only 16 times, while it refers to Jesus as Lord 420 times! Jesus himself insisted that anyone who wanted to become his disciple must take up his cross and follow him. And Paul and the rest of the New Testament make it crystal clear that accepting Christ as Lord means submitting every corner of one's life to him.

Many contemporary Christians act as if it is possible to divide Jesus up, accepting him as Savior and neglecting him as Lord. But Jesus Christ is one person. He cannot be torn apart in that way. Either we accept the whole person, Lord and Savior, or we do not accept him at all.

Throughout the Bible, we see God's people trying to separate their relationship with God from their relationships with neighbors. Always, God shouts a mighty no! The people of Israel thought they could worship God and oppress their neighbors. God's answer? "I hate, I despise your religious feasts. . . . But let justice roll on like a river" (Amos 5:21–24). Again and again, as we saw in the last chapter, Jesus insisted, "If you do not forgive others, neither will your Father forgive your trespasses" (Matt. 6:15 NRSV). If we say "Lord, Lord" but do not feed the hungry and clothe the naked, Jesus declared in Matthew 25 that we go to hell. Jesus is not teaching works righteousness. Our loving deeds for our neighbors do not earn divine acceptance. But Jesus is saying we must accept him as Lord as well as Savior.

The biblical teaching on conversion and discipleship constitutes two other ways the New Testament shows us that salvation is far more than merely forgiveness of sins.

The New Testament uses three Greek words to talk about repentance and conversion: *Epistrepho* literally means "to turn around." *Metanoia* (often translated "repentance") means "to change one's mind." *The Theological Dictionary of the New Testament* says *metanoia* demands an "unconditional turning from all that is against God" and an "unconditional turning to God."[13] The third word, *metamelomai*, means "to change one's mind." These three words point to the radical transformation of thoughts and actions that takes place when a person repents, accepts Christ as Lord and Savior, and experiences conversion.

Jesus said that the purpose of his coming was to call us to repentance (Luke 5:32). And Paul told the Corinthians that "godly sorrow brings repentance that leads to salvation" (2 Cor. 7:10). Repentance and conversion—turning in a whole new direction—are central to salvation.

In his masterful book *Dynamics of Spiritual Renewal*, Richard F. Lovelace offers a marvelous discussion about the importance of ongoing sanctification. He notes that the initial stage of coming to Christ "is not followed up with very searching instruction on the depth of the problem of residual indwelling sin, the subtlety of involvement in corporate patterns of sin and the grace of God available for the conquest of the flesh."[14] The result is congregations of born-again Christians that are not very alive spiritually. We need to recover the Puritans' emphasis on a lifetime of mortifying the sin that clings so tenaciously and subtly to us.

Jesus's final missionary mandate to us in Matthew 28:19 is to "make disciples." Making disciples is the basic command and two participles in the Greek text explain what it means: baptizing and teaching. We make disciples of Jesus by baptizing persons in the name of the Triune God *and* by "teaching them to obey everything I have commanded you" (v. 20). Again and again, Jesus made it clear that his disciples must be ready to give up absolutely everything—father, mother, sister, brother, property, even life itself. He said, "Whoever comes to me and does not hate father and mother, wife and children, brothers and sisters, yes, and even life itself, cannot be my disciple" (Luke 14:26 NRSV). Discipleship is at the very core of the salvation Jesus commands us to offer to the world. And discipleship means turning from sin and following Jesus as absolute, unconditional Lord.

Any notion that salvation is just forgiveness or that Christians can have justification without sanctification is as far from New Testament teaching as heaven is from hell. From the biblical perspective, forgiveness through the cross and transformation of our very character in sweeping conversion, submission to Christ as Lord of our whole being in obedient discipleship, and redeemed social and economic relationships in the community of believers are all part of the wonderful, full-orbed reality of salvation. If the church today grasps and embraces this biblical teaching on salvation, it will cry out to God for the grace and power to flee the scandal of its present disobedience.

Persons

Far too often, evangelicals think of persons primarily as individual souls. The really important part of a person is the soul. So we define evangelism as "saving souls."

That is flatly unbiblical. We have already seen that Jesus's gospel is far more than good news that individual souls can receive forgiveness and go to heaven. The gospel is the good news of the kingdom, and that kingdom includes the new social order that now in the power of the Spirit is becoming visible in the community of Christ's disciples. But adopting Jesus's definition of the gospel is only one part of the solution.

In the biblical understanding persons are far more than individual souls. Each person, as John Stott put it, is a "body-soul-in-community." It is the pagan philosopher Plato, not the biblical writers, who understood persons as primarily souls. Plato thought that each person had a good soul trapped in an evil body. The solution was for the soul to escape the body and be free. That unbiblical view led medieval Christians to a long litany of notions that belittled the body, considered sexual intercourse in marriage suspect if not positively sinful, and glorified asceticism. Modern evangelicalism's talk about "saving souls" stands in this long line of unbiblical confusion.

In the biblical framework, persons are soul and body: "God formed the man from the dust of the ground and breathed into his nostrils the breath of life, and the man became a living being" (Gen. 2:7). Human beings have a material part and a spiritual part, and the material part is very good. In fact, the body is so good that the Creator of 120 billion spinning galaxies became flesh, taking on a material body. In the flesh, he worked as a carpenter, sawing boards and hammering nails, thus sanctifying the physical world. In fact, the body is so good that Jesus rose bodily from the dead and promises to raise us to a renewed bodily existence at his second coming. The biblical promise is that when Christ returns, he will restore even the groaning creation to wholeness (Rom. 8:19–21) and welcome us to a glorious feast where we will delight in the good earth's bounty at the marriage supper of the Lamb. The future that Christians await is not some Platonic heaven where immaterial souls float around, but rather a transformed earth where resurrected bodies live. That is how good the body is.

It is true that many modern secular thinkers go to the other extreme from Christian Platonists. Marx, Darwin, and many contemporary secularists see persons as merely complex material machines. Nothing exists but the material world. That too is a fundamentally unbiblical understanding. Nothing in the material world, not even the entire material world, matters as much as our relationship with Christ (Matt. 16:24–26). Jesus insists that all who want to follow him must deny themselves and be willing to sacrifice even their very physical life: "For those who want to save their life will lose it, and those who lose their life for my sake will find it. For what will it profit them if they gain the whole world but forfeit their life?" (vv. 25–26 NRSV).

Understanding that we are made so that true life comes only when we are ready to give up material things, even physical life itself, frees us from materialism. The Creator made the material world good, wondrously good, but he also created persons so that nothing is as important to their well-being as a right relationship with God. Embracing this subtle biblical teaching on the goodness yet limitation of the material world will protect us from both Platonic asceticism and contemporary materialism.

In the biblical perspective, persons are both material and spiritual beings. That is why Jesus's gospel brings healing not just for souls but also for bodies. That is why the Scriptures constantly teach that God hates societies that oppress the poor and fail to provide opportunities for all to enjoy an abundant sufficiency of material goods. That is why the early church's dramatic economic sharing went hand in hand with its evangelistic proclamation. And that is why the great missionary to the Gentiles, Paul, spent many months taking up an intercontinental offering for poor Christians in Jerusalem (2 Cor. 8–9).

Persons are also communal beings. We are not made to be lone rangers or isolated hermits. We are created for community. Made in the image of the Triune God, a loving community of Father, Son, and Holy Spirit, we too are intended to live in relationship with others. That is clear from the fact that God made us males and females who need each other to reach God's intention for our lives. The first pair formed a family with children and they then began to work together to create civilizations. Born helpless, we simply die unless others care for us. Without others who pass on the inherited wisdom of human civilization, every person would have to invent everything anew. Without neighbors whose specialized knowledge and skills add immeasurably to the richness of our lives, we would live an incredibly barren existence. We simply cannot be who the Creator intended us to be as isolated individuals. We are made for community.

Western individualism largely ignores the communal aspect of human beings. Individual self-fulfillment becomes the highest value. The result is the destruction of covenantal family life and devastating neglect of our responsibility to our neighbors and the common good. One of the important reasons evangelical divorce rates are so high is that contemporary evangelicals unthinkingly adopt surrounding society's individualism. That same individualism nurtures consumeristic materialism and neglect of the poor. We desperately need to recover a biblical understanding of persons as body-soul unities made for community.

Sin

A couple decades ago it was a reasonably accurate generalization to say that evangelicals condemned personal sin and mainline Protestants denounced social sin. (By personal sin, I mean activities like lying, stealing, and committing adultery, and by social sin, I mean participating in unjust systems like slavery, apartheid, and economic injustice.)[15] Increasingly, however, pastors of every sort talk less and less about sin. Growing relativism, a fear of sounding "judgmental," a desire to be "seeker-friendly," and a psychologizing of sin all work against a clear biblical articulation of sin. As Cornelius Plantinga Jr. says, "Where sin is concerned, people mumble now."[16]

No one puts this more pointedly than the secular sociologist Alan Wolfe. Wolfe is an outside observer, an agnostic, whose recent book, *The Transformation of American Religion*, contains a brilliant analysis of contemporary American religion, especially evangelicalism. Wolfe thinks the widespread abandonment of the doctrine of sin is especially striking among evangelicals! He writes, "In no other area of religious practice, *especially for evangelicals*, is the gap between the religion as it is supposed to be and religion as it actually is as great as it is in the area of sin" (italics mine).[17] Even more striking, this self-confessed nonbeliever laments this "retreat from sin."

When it comes to sin, undoubtedly the first thing we need to do is recover the powerful biblical truth that our awesomely holy God hates sin. Evangelical preachers must rediscover how to preach about sin as clearly as the Bible does.

We also need to discover that in the Bible, sin is both personal and social. Again and again, the prophets make it perfectly clear that we sin both by lying, stealing, and committing adultery, and also by participating in unjust legal and economic systems without doing what God wants us to do to change them. Sin is both personal and social, so overcoming evil demands both personal and structural transformation.

But evangelicals still do not understand this. In his extensive research on American evangelicals, evangelical sociologist Chris Smith discovered that evangelicals today are just as engaged politically as mainline Protestants and Catholics. But when asked how society is changed, almost every evangelical responded that society is changed one person at a time. In his follow-up book on evangelicals and racism, Smith and his coauthor Michael O. Emerson discovered that evangelicals were dreadfully weak in their understanding of the structural causes of black-white inequality. When asked to explain the socioeconomic gap between black and white Americans, white evangelicals pointed largely to personal rather than structural causes. Sixty-two percent blamed lack of black motivation; only 27 percent blamed societal discrimination.[18] And the solution to racism? Again, evangelicals overwhelmingly chose personal approaches. Eighty-nine percent selected getting to know people of another race as the way to overcome racism. Only 38 percent chose racially integrating neighborhoods. In the years 1994–1998, twenty stories in *Christianity Today* advocated overcoming racism by getting to know a person of another race; only two talked of racially integrated neighborhoods.[19]

In its vigorous public call for overcoming racism, Promise Keepers took the same exclusively individualistic approach. They urged individual white men to befriend individual black men. Promise Keepers' chairman of the board insisted, "God moves in one heart at a time. The only way to change men [is] to change their hearts." One plenary speaker declared that racism is overcome not by "legislation but by relationships."[20]

This personal approach is *half* right! Sin is deeper than social structures. Sin *is* rooted in the human heart. Genuine conversion, unconditional submission to Christ as Lord, and eager openness to the transforming power of the Holy Spirit do dramatically change not only hearts but also outer behavior. It is partly because evangelicals engaged in evangelism see firsthand the dramatic transformation that personal conversion produces in mangled lives that we emphasize the importance of personal conversion. We dare never fall into the theologically liberal mistake of thinking that the only way to change society is via structural change.

But the evangelical approach is only half of the total solution. An exclusive emphasis on personal, individualistic approaches without a parallel concern for structural causes and solutions is wrong at several points: it contradicts our present political activity, it ignores our past success in changing structures, it is inconsistent with the biblical understanding of persons, and it totally ignores the biblical teaching on social sin.

Evangelicals today are deeply engaged in political activity to protect the family and the sanctity of human life. I support these efforts. But do we say that since the only way to change society is one person at a time, we should not try to pass laws protecting marriage and the sanctity of human life? Do we say that we should spend all our efforts trying to befriend pregnant teenagers and convert the sexually promiscuous? Not at all. We rightly seek to make abortion-on-demand illegal. We rightly seek an amendment to the U.S. Constitution to define marriage as exclusively between a man and a woman. These are structural solutions to social problems—but they do not fit with the idea that we change society just "one person at a time."

Wilberforce and other evangelical abolitionists took the same systemic approach to ending slavery. They did not argue that the only way to end slavery was to convert all the slave owners. They worked for new laws that would change the structures by making slaveholding illegal.

The biblical understanding of persons provides the foundation for the approach to overcoming evil that combines both personal and also structural change. Persons are responsible individuals who make wrong choices. Therefore, converting sinners so they start to make good choices is a central part of how to correct societal brokenness. As we saw earlier, however, persons are also communal beings. We live in families and communities that profoundly influence our behavior. The Bible says, "Train children in the right way, and when old, they will not stray" (Prov. 22:6 NRSV). Societal influences have a profound impact on people in one direction or another. That is why evangelicals rightly resist sending their children to schools that teach relativism, affirm wrong sexual values, and encourage children to hang out with drug users. Bad structures foster immoral behavior. Good systems encourage moral actions. The Creator made us communal beings who are influenced by the persons and systems that surround us. If we understand this, we will work to overcome racism and economic injustice through both personal and structural strategies.

Probably the clearest way the Bible points to this both/and approach is in its teaching that sin is both personal and social. The prophets regularly denounced social sin as well as personal sin. Amos 2:6–7 is a classic example.[21]

> They sell the righteous for silver,
>   and the needy for a pair of sandals.
> They trample on the heads of the poor
>   as upon the dust of the ground
>   and deny justice to the oppressed.
> Father and son use the same girl
>   And so profane my holy name.

Most of this text denounces economic oppression. Scholars point out that the "righteous" person who is sold for silver or sandals is a poor person with a good legal case, but the rich and powerful bribe the judges and win. Corrupt legal systems result in gross economic injustice. But then the last two lines condemn sexual misconduct (perhaps cult prostitution). God abhors both sexual sin and economic oppression.

Amos 5:10–12 continues the attack against unfair structures—in this case an oppressive legal system supporting oppressive economic structures:

> You hate the one who reproves in court
>   and despise him who tells the truth.
> You trample on the poor
>   and force him to give you grain. . . .
> You oppress the righteous and take bribes
>   and you deprive the poor of justice in the courts.

Isaiah fulminates against legislators and bureaucrats who write and implement oppressive laws (Isa. 10:1–4). And the psalmist insists that God will wipe out those who "frame mischief by statute" (Ps. 94:20 RSV).

Amos 4:1–2 shows that we sin against God and neighbor when we choose to participate in unjust systems. Amos denounced the wealthy women of his day because they encouraged and participated in the oppressive economic and judicial structures that brought them wealth.

> Hear this word, you cows of Bashan on Mount
>   Samaria,
> you women who oppress the poor and crush the needy
>   and say to your husbands, "Bring us some drinks!"
> The Sovereign LORD has sworn by his holiness:

"The time will surely come
when you will be taken away with hooks,
   the last of you with fishhooks."

Amos predicted that a foreign nation would conquer Israel, tear down their cities, and drag the wealthy women away by the nose. Because they chose to participate in and benefit from oppressive structures, God brought terrible punishment on these affluent women.

In the New Testament, the word *cosmos* (world) often conveys the idea of structural evil. In Greek thought, the word *cosmos* referred to the structures of civilized life, especially the patterns of the Greek city-state that were viewed by many as essentially good. But the biblical writers knew that sin had invaded and distorted the structures and values of society.

Frequently, therefore, the New Testament uses the word *cosmos* to refer, in C. H. Dodd's words, "to human society in so far as it is organized on wrong principles."[22] Dodd writes, "When Paul spoke of 'the world' in a moral sense, he was thinking of the totality of people, social systems, values, and traditions in terms of its opposition to God and his redemptive purposes."[23] Before conversion, Christians followed the values and patterns of a fallen social order. "You were dead in your transgressions and sins," Paul writes to the Ephesians, "in which you used to live when you followed the ways of this world" (2:1–2). Paul and John urge Christians not to conform to this world's pattern of evil systems and ideas, as the following passages testify:

Do not be conformed to this world, but be transformed
by the renewing of your minds, so that you may discern
what is the will of God—what is good and acceptable and
perfect.

Romans 12:2 NRSV

Do not love the world or the things in the world. The love of
the Father is not in those who love the world; for all that is
in the world—the desire of the flesh, the desire of the eyes,
the pride in riches—comes not from the Father but from
the world. And the world and its desire are passing away,
but those who do the will of God live forever.

1 John 2:15–17 NRSV

Behind the distorted social structures of our world, according to St. Paul, are fallen supernatural powers under
the control of Satan himself. When Paul says that, before
the Ephesians' conversion, they had "followed the ways
of this world," he adds, "and of the ruler of the kingdom
of the air, the spirit who is now at work in those who are
disobedient" (Eph. 2:2). Paul warns that "our struggle is
not against flesh and blood, but against the rulers, against
the authorities, against the powers of this dark world and
against the spiritual forces of evil in the heavenly realms"
(Eph. 6:12).

Both Jews and Greeks in Paul's day believed that both
good and evil supernatural beings stand behind and powerfully influence social and political structures. Modern
secular folk may find that hard to believe. But when I look
at the demonic evil of social systems like Nazism, apartheid,
and communism, or even the complex mixture of racism,

lack of jobs, sexual promiscuity, drugs, and police brutality in American inner cities, I have no trouble at all believing that Satan and his gang are hard at work fostering oppressive structures and thus doing their best to destroy God's good creation.

These fallen supernatural powers work to twist and distort the social systems that we as social beings need in order to be whole. By seducing us into many wrong choices that create evil systems, by working against attempts to overcome oppressive structures and sometimes by enticing politicians and other powerful leaders to use the occult, these demonic powers shape our world. Evil is far more complex than the wrong choices of individuals. It also lies outside us both in powerfully oppressive social systems and in demonic powers that delight in defying God by corrupting the social systems that God's human image-bearers need.

Pope John Paul II has rightly insisted that evil social structures are "rooted in personal sin." Social evil results from our rebellion against God and our consequent selfishness toward our neighbors. But he goes on to say that the "accumulation and concentration of many *personal sins*" create evil social structures that are both "oppressive and difficult to change."[24] When we choose to participate in and benefit from evil social systems, as did the affluent women of Amos's time, we sin against God and neighbor.

One of the most striking illustrations of evangelical failure to understand social evil appeared in the special forum *Christianity Today* organized to respond to Emerson and Smith's *Divided by Faith*, which argued that evangelicalism actually contributed to racial division. Even though Emerson and Smith placed a significant part of the blame on evangelicals' lack of understanding of structural injustice, not a single evangelical leader on the *Christianity Today* forum responded by urging that evangelicals recover the clear biblical teaching on social sin![25]

Unless we embrace the biblical truth that sin is personal and social, we will never understand either the full set of causes or a comprehensive set of solutions to racism and economic injustice—or, for that matter, the destruction of the family and the loss of respect for the sanctity of human life. Because of the way God made us, we change society *both* one person at a time and through changing unjust systems. A biblical perspective demands both personal conversion and structural change.

A couple decades ago, an Indian bishop told me the following story to underline the importance of structural change. There was once an Indian hospital for the mentally ill which had a very interesting way of determining whether a person was sane enough to return home. The hospital staff would begin to fill a large basin with water and give a spoon to the person whose sanity was in question. Then, as the water continued to flow into the basin, the staff asked the person to empty the basin with the spoon. If the person started dipping the water out of the basin one spoonful at a time without first turning the tap off, they knew the person was still crazy.

Until evangelicals grasp the biblical teaching that sin is social as well as personal, we will continue with our foolishly one-sided solutions to today's complex social problems.

In this chapter, we have seen how evangelical theology is genuinely unbiblical at important points. A full-orbed biblical understanding of the gospel, salvation, persons, and sin would help us live more faithfully. This is not to suggest that theological changes by themselves would solve our problems. But greater biblical fidelity would help end the scandal.

Conforming to Culture or Being the Church

Watching over one another in love.

John Wesley

American popular culture is sick, sick unto death. And the illness has swept through the church. Hollywood's outrageous sexual values and crazy consumerism are rooted in pervasive, long-standing individualism and materialism that have taken deep root in our culture. Tragically, not even the evangelical community has effectively resisted popular culture's corrosive influence. What early generations of evangelicals, whether Calvinists, Methodists, Anabaptists, or Pentecostals, assumed and embraced about mutual responsibility and accountability in the body of Christ has largely been lost. The gospel of individual self-fulfillment now reigns.

We all know that many of Hollywood's values, projected globally with enticing power, are fundamentally destructive. Two-day marriages, constant divorces, and adulterous affairs are standard fare for our TV and movie idols. Their TV shows and successful movies make sexual fidelity and lifelong marriage appear boring, old-fashioned, and silly.

Disgusting, albeit titillating, reality-TV shows sweep the ratings. Everywhere, seductive advertising urges us to buy more cosmetics, potions, and gadgets to guarantee instant joy and personal fulfillment. Knowing that this is what American media exports all around the world makes one realize why many people in other countries despise America.

Conforming to Culture

Behind this sick popular culture is a long history of growing individualism and materialism rooted in the Enlightenment's abandonment of historic Christian theism. For almost fifteen hundred years, Western civilization had been grounded in a shared conviction that God, at the center of reality, was the source of moral norms, governmental authority, truth, and beauty. But in the eighteenth century leading thinkers began to argue that the ever more successful scientific project would make the "hypothesis" of God unnecessary. Nothing exists except the material world described with ever-greater scientific precision. The individual replaced God at the center of reality.

At first, thinkers like the philosopher Immanuel Kant thought that human reason could be the source of a universal

86

ethic. But then Charles Darwin argued that all that exists is merely the result of a blind evolutionary process. Ethical and religious ideas are merely subjective notions that enable the fittest to survive. Then Karl Marx persuaded many that all our thoughts, including our ethical and religious ideas, are simply the product of economic forces. In the early twentieth century, Freud explained away religion and ethics as the result of infantile needs and projections. A widespread pervasive relativism spread throughout the intellectual world. Nothing was left but the lonely individual arbitrarily creating subjective meaning for himself or herself.

For a time, this relativism remained largely confined to elite academic and intellectual circles. But in the revolution of the sixties, the radical ideas spread quickly throughout the larger culture. Self-fulfillment for the sovereign individual became the highest value. Pop psychology taught that you should choose whatever you personally felt would contribute to your personal happiness. If your spouse was not meeting your "needs," you owed it to yourself to find someone else who would. If you did not, you would probably do something awful to your psyche. Society cast aside historic Christian ethical norms. The media glamorized promiscuity. No-fault divorce laws swept through legislatures. The result has been escalating divorce, soaring out-of-wedlock birth rates, a vast expansion of single parenthood, broken families, and widespread pain and agony in our homes.

In the last couple decades, postmodernism has heightened the relativism. Postmodernists reduce all ethical norms and truth claims to the self-centered power games of groups, races, and classes. Nothing is true or right. All statements are simply the product of some group's or class's desire to dominate others for their own selfish advantage.

A prevailing belief in the West today is that whatever feels right for me is right for me and whatever feels right for you is right for you. The only unpardonable sin is to claim that absolute right and wrong exist and that a person's personal choices are immoral. Relativism has conquered.

At the same time, a new kind of materialism has taken root. Historic Christianity had been profoundly materialistic. The created world is good. God wants us to create wealth and delight in the bounty of the material world. But historic Christianity also placed firm boundaries on this materialism. Nothing, not even the whole material world, matters as much as one's relationship with God. The Sabbath reminded people that once every seven days we should forget productive work and focus especially on worship of God. Happiness comes first of all not from material things, but from right relationships with God and neighbor, and then thirdly from a generous sufficiency of material things.

Then Darwin convinced the intellectual world that the entire history of life on this planet is simply the result of blind material forces accidentally producing chance mutations that through natural selection produce evolutionary change. Nothing exists but the material world, which we can count and measure. One cannot easily measure love and justice, but one can measure annual income and gross domestic product. People focused more and more on accumulating material things—a perfectly good decision if, finally, nothing else exists. The boundaries that historic Christianity had placed on materialism fell away. Material abundance and self-fulfillment through more and more things became the highest values.

Meanwhile the stunning success of market economies in producing ever-greater material abundance nurtured a practical materialism that has maximized individual choice. Desiring ever-growing sales to produce ever-greater profits, businesses discovered the power of seductive advertising. Ever more subtle ads persuaded ever more self-centered materialists that the way to joy and fulfillment was via greater and greater material abundance. A very effective ad produced by a prominent Philadelphian bank used the big lie that love comes from material things like a bank account. "Put a little love away," ran the ad. "Everybody needs a penny for a rainy day." Thirty years later, I can still remember the slogan.

Working harder to earn more money to buy ever-bigger houses and more sophisticated gadgets and cars became the national passion. Regardless of the fact that 86 percent of Americans continue to tell pollsters that they believe in God, they have become practical materialists. Gaining more wealth and material things has become more important than spending time with one's children, spouse, or church community.

Stunning technological breakthroughs and expanding material abundance heightened the individualism. Medical advances made it medically "safe" for individuals to choose easy abortions when a child seemed inconvenient. New birth control devices brought "safe sex," which encouraged sexual promiscuity. Companies manufactured an ever-greater range of products and paid the advertisers to appeal to the personal choice of sovereign individuals.

Everyone was urged to choose this or that new thing in order to be happy. Personal choice of more and more little pleasures and gadgets reigned supreme.

Peter Gillquist summarizes the result of this preoccupation with personal choice and self-fulfillment: "We have become such a nation of self-lovers. Nothing is too sacred to leave—if we feel like it. We leave school if it gets boring or difficult; we leave home and parents if we're displeased; we leave our jobs, our marriages, and our churches."[1]

Tragically the Christian church, including the evangelical community, was unable to resist this tide of relativism, materialism, and individualism. Relativism has invaded evangelical thinking. Barna reports that his national surveys show that *only 14 percent* of born-again adults "rely on the Bible as their moral compass *and* believe that moral truth is absolute."[2] We abandoned the Sabbath with its weekly reminder that God matters more than production. Church leaders and theologians produced simplistic gospels of wealth or more sophisticated justifications of "godly materialism" to sanctify evangelicals' increasing preoccupation with material abundance. The richer we became, the less we gave to the church and the poor. Parents focused on growing salaries, neglecting their children. Successful professionals worked long hours even if it destroyed their marriages.

The pastor of an Evangelical Covenant congregation shared with me a few years ago one of the most striking illustrations of how society's relativism is invading the minds of evangelical youth. For the previous six years, at the end of a multiweek catechetical class preparing his teenagers for church membership, my friend had conducted a fascinating experiment.

First, he placed a jar of marbles in front of the class. "How many marbles are in the jar?" he asked. The youngsters responded with different guesses: 150, 143, 177, and so on. He responded, "Well, I counted them and there are exactly 157 marbles in the jar. Now, which of your answers was closest to being right?" And they agreed it was the answer closest to 157. "Of course," he concluded, "the quantity of marbles is a matter of fact, not personal opinion."

Then he asked what their favorite songs were. As different persons named different songs, he wrote them on the blackboard. He then asked, "Which is the right song?" As expected, everyone said this was an unfair question because each person's preference was right for him- or herself. "Exactly," he concluded, "the right song has to do with a person's musical tastes. It is a matter of personal opinion, not fact."

He concluded the experiment by talking about the deity of Jesus Christ and his resurrection on the third day, reminding them that some people doubt both. He then said to them, "Now, are the deity of Jesus Christ and his resurrection matters of fact, or are they matters of personal opinion? Are they like the question about the number of marbles or like the question of which music you prefer?" Sadly, he told me, every youngster for six years said the deity and resurrection of Christ are like the question about the music—mere matters of personal opinion.

Everywhere, individualism has conquered evangelical traditions of accountability in the church. Denominations that for decades and even centuries had practiced mutual accountability in the church through church discipline quickly abandoned the practice. When I joined the church in my evangelical denomination as a young teenager, the ritual for church membership included the promise that I would practice and submit to church discipline as taught by Jesus in Matthew 18:15–17. That ritual has disappeared. In fact, in one congregation I know in my evangelical denomination, a man and a woman from two different married couples had an affair, divorced their spouses, married each other, and assumed they could continue in good standing in the congregation in spite of their defiance of Jesus's teaching and the destruction of two families. Not even in this blatant case of stark disobedience could this evangelical congregation muster the courage to exercise church discipline.

Gillquist says we now have "churchless born-againism"—a new type of apostasy that he says has never appeared before in history. "This movement," he writes, "confesses a personal—really, *private*—relationship with Christ and denies the Lordship of Christ as being in the church. Christ, they say, rules *only in one's heart*, and thus they end up despising God's ordained government. This view floods our modern para-church movements."[3]

Individualism is pervasive in the evangelical world. We now pick and choose—and switch—churches almost as quickly as we select or change brands in the supermarket or channels on TV. Independent congregations are accountable to no one but themselves. Independent evangelical parachurch organizations have almost no accountability to the larger church. Dominant, "successful" senior pastors can do almost anything they please.

Three incidents illustrate the individualism.

1. When Tammy Faye was cohost of a very popular evangelical TV program with her husband, Jim Bakker,

she wrote a book called *I Gotta Be Me*.[4] Whatever happened to sacrificing self for the sake of Christ?

2. A prominent Baptist leader defended the total independence of the individual Christian from any larger church accountability with the words "Ain't nobody but Jesus gonna tell me what to do."

3. And Robert Schuller announced a Gospel of Self-Esteem. "The gospel of Jesus Christ," he wrote, "can be proclaimed as a theology of self-esteem."[5]

Individualism creeps into the best of our contemporary Christian songs. I deeply love and regularly feel a surge of genuine religious emotion as I sing "As the Deer Panteth for the Waters." It is a simply wonderful song about the fact that God must be the absolute center of our lives. But one of the lines says, "You alone are my strength and shield, to you alone doth my spirit yield." Oops. Should I not listen carefully and indeed yield to other mature brothers and sisters in the body of Christ? Am I supposed to listen only to what I hear Christ saying and not submit to other Christians? Fewer and fewer evangelicals today do submit to others. If our local church does not meet our needs and offer what feels good to us, we simply move on to another congregation.

Being the Church

Few things are more urgent today than a recovery of the New Testament understanding and practice of the church.[6] According to the first Christians, Jesus expects the church to be his holy community living according to biblical norms rather than worldly values. How can we do that? Through mutual accountability and the power of the Spirit.

Six points are crucial. First, Jesus is the source, center, and Lord of the church. Second, the church is holy. Third, it is a community, not a collection of lone rangers. Fourth, precisely because it submits to Jesus's kingdom norms, the church is a countercultural community living a lifestyle that fundamentally challenges worldly values and practices. Fifth, mutual accountability and responsibility are essential in this astonishing new social order. Sixth, only in the power of the Spirit is it possible for this new community to be the new righteous, countercultural social order that its Lord requires.

Jesus Is the Center

The church came into being through God's initiative in Christ. It exists only because Jesus came, lived among us, died for our sins, and rose from the dead. The church is now the body *of Christ*, and he is its head (Eph. 4:12, 15). New believers enter the church through baptism into Christ. All Christians enjoy the regular renewal that comes through the Lord's Supper, which reminds us of his death for us and points us toward his promised return (1 Cor. 11:25–26). Central to the church's mission is the call to share Jesus's gospel and invite non-Christians to embrace the Good News and join Jesus's new community. There is one Lord, one faith, one baptism, one body (Eph. 4:1–5). Wherever one looks, Jesus Christ is at the very core of everything the New Testament says about the church.

The Church Is Called to Be Holy

The very purpose of Christ's coming to earth, the New Testament declares, was to create a holy community: Christ "gave himself for us to redeem us from all wickedness and to *purify for himself a people* that are his very own, eager to do what is good" (Titus 2:14, italics mine). St. Paul also insists that Christ came precisely to create a holy church: "Christ loved the church and gave himself up for her to make her holy, cleansing her by the washing with water through the word, and to present her to himself as a radiant church, without stain or wrinkle or any other blemish, but holy and blameless" (Eph. 5:25–27). Peter commands the Christians not to conform to their former sinful ways but rather to live in holiness: "Just as he who called you is holy, so be holy in all you do; for it is written: 'Be holy, because I am holy'" (1 Peter 1:14–16). At the end of vigorous ethical instruction to the church at Corinth, Paul issues the ringing summons, "Let us purify ourselves from everything that contaminates body and spirit, perfecting holiness out of reverence for God" (2 Cor. 7:1).

The New Testament uses the images of the church as virgin and bride to underline an expectation that the church will be holy. In the parable of the virgins, Jesus describes those who enter the kingdom as virgins waiting in eager expectation and full preparation for the bridegroom (Matt. 25:1–13). Paul tells the Corinthian Christians that he wants to present them as "pure virgins" to be the bride of Christ (2 Cor. 11:1–2). Repeatedly, in the final chapters of Revelation, we see the church described as the bride of Christ

(19:7–8; 21:2, 8). Purity and holiness are at the core of these images of the church as virgin and bride.

Increasingly today, evangelicals repeat the Apostles' Creed with its clear confession of the church as holy. But our lifestyles contradict our confession. Our disobedient lifestyles crucify our Lord anew.

The Church as Community

As in the time of the judges in Israel, so it is in the church today. Each person does what is good in his or her own eyes. If Christians today could recover even half of the profound New Testament understanding of the church as community, we would discover a powerful protection against the pervasive individualism that devastates the Western church.

The ultimate foundation of Christian community is our Triune God. The one God, who is a loving community of Father, Son, and Holy Spirit, created us in the divine image. Community, therefore, is an essential part of what it means to be human. Unfortunately, sin sent shock waves of devastation through all human communities. But the Creator who is the Redeemer resolved to restore the goodness of human community that Satan had corrupted. The people of Israel and then the church were to be God's demonstration projects.

In his final prayer for the church, Jesus shows us that God wants the kind of communal love that exists in the Trinity to find a parallel in the loving community of Jesus's disciples.[7] Jesus prayed "that all of them [i.e., the church] may be one, Father, just as you are in me and I am in you" (John 17:21). When we say with the late activist and evangelist Tom Skinner that the church today should be a little picture of what heaven will be like, we mean in part that when at Christ's return the church fully expresses the complete righteousness that God desires, it finally also will be a truly accurate image of the Triune God.

God's grand strategy of redemption does not focus on redeeming isolated individuals; it centers on the creation of a new people, a new community, a new social order that begins to live now the way the Creator intended. That is clear all through the Scriptures, from the calling of Israel out of Egypt to the final book of the Bible. When God called Moses to lead the Israelites out of Egypt, God promised, "I will take you as my own people" (Exod. 6:7). Not as my own individuals! As a community the Israelites were God's people. And God gave them laws to show them how to live well together in community: The judicial system must be fair. The economic arrangements must enable each family to earn a generous sufficiency. And there must be special attention to the poor, widows, and orphans—those who lose their place in the community through poverty or death of a husband or father.

Jesus was not a lone ranger who made private house calls on isolated hermits or autonomous individuals. Jesus gathered a circle of disciples and together they formed a new community. The earliest Christians in Jerusalem understood their oneness in Christ and therefore their mutual responsibility to each other to include sweeping economic sharing within the new Christian community. St. Paul the evangelist devoted much of his time over the course of several years to collecting a big offering for the poor Christians in Jerusalem. This striking intercontinental offering demonstrated the unity of the global Christian community. And when God brings down the curtain on history as we know it, God himself will come to dwell in the midst of the community he has formed: "He will live with them. They will be his *people*" (Rev. 21:3, italics mine).

The three most common images of the church in the New Testament—the people of God, the family of God, and the body of Christ—all emphasize the communal character of the church.

When the New Testament writers describe the church as the people of God, the idea of Israel as God's chosen people is always present. That is especially clear in 1 Peter 2:9–10:

> But you are a chosen people, a royal priesthood, a holy nation, a people belonging to God, that you may declare the praises of him who called you out of darkness into his wonderful light. Once you were not a people, but now you are the people of God; once you had not received mercy, but now you have received mercy.

The key words here are communal words. The church is a people, a nation. Peter alludes to the prophetic promise (Hosea 2:23) that sometime in the future, after the terrible punishment of Israel for her sins by partially rejecting her as his people, God would restore Israel as his chosen people. Peter applies that promise to the church. God's promise to restore Israel is now being fulfilled in the new Christian community.

The numerous references to the church as the "Israel of God" make the same point (Gal. 6:16; Eph. 2:12; Heb. 8:8–10). So do the passages on Christians as Abraham's sons and daughters (Rom. 4:16; Gal. 3:29). To describe the church as the people of God, the Israel of God, and the children of Abraham is to emphasize powerfully the communal nature of the church.

The frequently used image of the church as the "family of God" has the same impact. Christians are sons and daughters of God, who is the Father of this family (Gal. 4:4–7). As children of God the Father, Christians are co-heirs with Christ: "The Spirit himself testifies with our spirit that we are God's children. Now if we are children, then we are heirs—heirs of God and co-heirs with Christ" (Rom. 8:16–17). Christ, the unique Son of God, is also our brother in this family of God (Heb. 2:10–13).

One of the most striking illustrations of the church as family is the fact that the words "brother" and "brothers" became the most common form of greeting among the early Christians. Everywhere in the New Testament we see Christians addressing each other as "brothers." Peter in fact says the church is one worldwide brotherhood (1 Peter 5:9).

This new brotherhood and sisterhood in the family of God cuts across all natural, human ties. Jesus explicitly taught that our loyalty to the new family of God must exceed our commitment to natural family ties to father, mother, sister, and brother. When it does, we receive new brothers and sisters by the hundreds! (See Mark 10:29–30.) This new family is based not on biological relationships but on faith (Gal. 4) and doing the will of God. Jesus insisted, "Whoever does God's will is my brother and sister and mother" (Mark 3:35).

The image of the church as family underlines several things. First it clearly teaches that our relationship with

God (whom Jesus, our brother, taught us to call "Papa") is a personal, intimate relationship. Equally intimate is our relationship with the other members of this family. Also important is the fact that our identity in this new family of the church transcends (although it does not replace or cancel) natural family ties.

This image also points to the fact that we do not personally choose who else belongs to the family. God the Father makes that decision. We are "stuck" with the rest of the family whether or not we have warm, fuzzy feelings about them. God the Father simply calls all kinds of people—Jew and Gentile, male and female, educated and uneducated, master and slave, rich and poor—into his family and demands that his children embrace them all as their very own sisters and brothers.

Finally, this image is an incredibly powerful way of saying that the church is a body, a social order, a communal reality. It is a community of mutual love, sharing, and accountability.

Perhaps Paul's fantastic image of the church as the body of Christ is the most powerful of all the communal images of the church. First Corinthians 12–14 and Ephesians 4:11–16 are the most important texts.

Paul uses the analogy of the human body to resolve disputes in the Corinthian church about the relative importance of different spiritual gifts (1 Corinthians 12). Every part of the human body is important. It would be absurd for the hand to declare its independence and announce that it no longer needs the services of the eye or foot. So too the church as the spiritual body of Christ needs every member. God designed this body so that "its parts should have equal concern for each other." In fact, "if one part suffers, every part suffers with it; if one part is honored, every part rejoices with it" (vv. 25–26). So too in the body of Christ, every individual matters and everyone shares in the joys and sorrows of all the others. The special gifts of each are for the blessing of the whole body of Christ.

Again, in Ephesians 4, St. Paul talks about the way the different spiritual gifts work together "so that the body of Christ may be built up until we all reach unity in the faith and in the knowledge of the Son of God and become mature, attaining to the whole measure of the fullness of Christ" (vv. 12–13). What a goal! Every Christian in the body of Christ is to become (fully!) like Christ. That happens only as each part of the body submits to Christ its head: "From him the whole body, joined and held together by every supporting ligament, grows and builds itself up in love, as each part does its work" (v. 16).

This image fairly screams the theological truth that the unity of the body of Christ is grounded not in some common sociological identity of race, class, or blood but only in Christ's act of redemption. We share in one baptism and one Lord's Supper, and that makes us one. Period. "Because there is one loaf, we, who are many, are one body, for we all partake of the one loaf" (1 Cor. 10:17). Whether it feels good or not, we are stuck with those sociological "others" in the church. Racial or social discrimination in the church is a fundamental denial of the very meaning of the oneness of Christ's body.

In fact, as we saw in chapter 2, the multiethnic body of believers is part of the gospel Paul proclaims. Jesus's gospel of the kingdom—the Good News that the new messianic social order promised by the prophets is now breaking into history—became a visible, living reality as Jews accepted Gentiles, men accepted women, and masters accepted slaves as full members of the one body of Christ. The gospel became flesh as the Jerusalem church placed the entire program of financial assistance to all widows in the hands of the ethnic Grecian minority whose widows had been neglected (Acts 6). The early church looked forward to that glorious day when they would be part of "a great multitude that no one could count, from every nation, tribe, people and language, standing before the throne and in front of the Lamb" (Rev. 7:9). But they did not just dream about it in the future. They lived it in the present because they understood what it meant for the church to be the one body of Christ.

Paul is explicit about the communal implications of his doctrine of the church as the body of Christ. It means sharing each other's joys and sorrows. And that includes—as Paul's teaching on the intercontinental offering for poor Christians in Jerusalem demonstrates—economic sharing with other sisters and brothers. Being one body also means being responsible for each other's spiritual growth. He says explicitly that the various gifts of the one body are so that every member of the body reaches maturity in Christ. That is why Paul insists in Galatians that "if someone is caught in a sin, you who are spiritual should restore him gently" (6:1). The church is one vast community of mutual accountability and responsibility.

If we grasp the New Testament understanding of the church, then we realize that the modern, evangelical reduction of Christianity to some personal, privatized affair that only affects my personal relationship with God and perhaps my personal family life is blatant heresy. The church is a new, visible social order. It is a radical new community visibly living a challenge to the sexual insanity, the racial and social prejudice, and the economic injustice that pervade the rest of society. The church, as Rodney Clapp says so well in *A Peculiar People*, is a new way of living together in community.[8] It *is* community—Jesus's new messianic community.

British evangelical Michael Green powerfully captures this reality of the church as a new kind of community.

> They made the grace of God credible by a society of love and mutual care which astonished pagans and was recognized as something entirely new. It lent persuasiveness to the claim that the new age had dawned in those who were giving it flesh. The message of the kingdom became more than an idea. A new human community had sprung up and looked very much like the new order to which the evangelist had pointed. Here love was given daily expression; reconciliation was actually occurring; people were no longer divided into Jews and Gentiles, slave and free, male and female. In this community the weak were protected, the stranger welcomed. People were healed, the poor and dispossessed were cared for and found justice. Almost everything was shared. Joy abounded and ordinary lives were filled with praise.[9]

A Countercultural Community

If the church is truly a visible social order that lives like Jesus rather than the world, if the church is a community that understands that Jesus's challenge to what was wrong in the status quo was part of his proclamation of the gospel of the kingdom, if the church seeks to be a visible manifestation of Jesus's dawning kingdom rather than a carbon copy of the fallen world which is passing away, then the church inevitably is profoundly countercultural. That is not because culture itself is bad. Culture is part of God's good creation. The Creator made us in his very image and called us to use the material world he gave us to create tools; art; music; and complex, beautiful civilizations. All that is good. But the fall messed up everything. Sin has permeated every corner of culture. Therefore, Jesus's people, precisely because we love and embrace the gorgeous creation the Creator gave us and therefore want to shape new splendid cultural creations to the glory of God, must say no to all that is sinful and distorted in surrounding culture. Precisely because we love culture, we must be countercultural. Precisely because we follow Jesus, our churches must be loving disrupters of the sinful status quo rather than comfortable clubs of conformity.

This call to be a countercultural community runs all through the New Testament. Jesus warned that the world would hate his followers because they refused to live like the world. The New Testament writers used the images of aliens and strangers to describe the church. "Dear friends," Peter writes, "I urge you, as aliens and strangers in the world, to abstain from sinful desires" (1 Peter 2:11; also Heb. 11:13–16). Nobody puts it more powerfully than St. Paul: "Do not conform any longer to the pattern of this world, but be transformed by the renewing of your mind" (Rom. 12:2). "Come out from them and be separate," Paul urges in another vigorous call for separation from the sin of the world (2 Cor. 6:17).

Stanley Hauerwas and William H. Willimon capture this biblical teaching very effectively in their book *Resident Aliens*. In a crucial sense this modern world is not our home. The church should be "a colony . . . a beachhead, an outpost, an island of one culture in the middle of another, a place where the values of home are reiterated and passed on to the young, a place where the distinctive language and lifestyle of resident aliens are lovingly nurtured and reinforced."[10]

It is absolutely essential that the church today recover this biblical sense of the church as a countercultural community living separate from the sin of the world. A couple generations ago, evangelicals did have a sense of their separation from the world. Author Tom Sine remembers that time: "When I attended an evangelical Christian college in the fifties, everyone knew what would derail a vital faith: 'worldliness.' Therefore the way to maintain a vital Christian life was simply to abstain from worldliness."[11] Unfortunately, we often misunderstood worldliness in petty, legalistic ways, condemning cosmetics, dancing, card playing, or in my tradition wearing neckties!

Tragically, much of contemporary evangelicalism has abandoned not just petty legalisms but biblical substance as well. The radical worldliness that pervades surrounding society has infiltrated almost every part of the church. This worldliness takes the forms of racism, sexual promiscuity, materialism, and easy divorce. Biblical Christians will not separate themselves from the hurting people who do such things. Confused wanderers desperately need loving Christians who can point them to the Savior and love them into the kingdom. But biblical Christians will separate themselves from destructive sinful behavior. We must nurture a new community of transformed sinners whose common life is so faithful to Jesus that it stands in stark contrast to the tragic brokenness of surrounding society. We simply cannot follow Jesus in this crazy society unless we recover a deep sense of the church as a countercultural community.

Indeed, the church ought to be not just different but far ahead of the rest of society. In light of what the New Testament says about the multiethnic character of the church, Christian congregations today should be far ahead instead of lagging behind the rest of society in the struggle against racism. In light of what the New Testament says about economic sharing in the one body of Christ, the church should stand out in stunning contrast to surrounding materialism as Christians give 10, 20, 30 percent and more of their income to do the work of the kingdom, including empowering Christians and others to escape poverty. In light of what the Bible says about sexual purity and marital fidelity, the love and joy in Christian homes where spouses keep their vows for a lifetime should contrast so starkly with the agony in contemporary families that millions of broken persons are attracted to the Savior.

Mutual Accountability and Availability

If the church is an intimate community, indeed a family, then the members of that community must be accountable to each other and be available to each other. This includes both our economic and spiritual lives.

In both the Old Testament and the New, Scripture makes it abundantly clear that a central part of what it means to be

God's special people is to experience redeemed economic relationships in that community. When the Israelites enter the land of Canaan, God directs them to divide the land so that every family has enough land to earn a generous sufficiency. Then God adds the striking law that every fifty years, land must return to the original landowner (Leviticus 25). Numerous other laws require that God's people show special concern for the poor and needy in their midst.

Dramatic economic sharing among God's people continues in the New Testament. Jesus said that the economic sharing among his disciples would be so extensive that everyone would enjoy a hundred times more houses and lands (Mark 10:29–30). The earliest Jerusalem Christians shared so deeply that "there were no needy persons among them" (Acts 4:34). And Paul, as we have seen, devoted much time to a large, intercontinental offering to demonstrate economic fellowship in the one body of Christ. He even insisted that when rich Corinthian Christians refused to share their abundance with poor Christians at the Lord's Supper, they destroyed the very essence of the sacrament. By their refusal to share their abundance, they were denying the oneness of the body of Christ (1 Cor. 11:29).

Mutual accountability for spiritual growth was also central to the life of the early church. Paul called them to share each other's joys and sorrows. He commanded the spiritually mature to correct those who fell into sin. He demanded that the Corinthian church expel a member who persisted in sin. They implemented their belief that the purpose of the spiritual gifts given to individual members was to build up the whole body so that all members come to maturity in Christ.

107

Paul actually summoned Christians to be slaves to each other. That is what Galatians 5:13 literally says. The standard translation, "serve one another in love," masks the radical demand. But the key word here is the word for *slave*. "Be slaves to each other" would be an accurate literal translation. This is the level of availability that membership in Christ's body demands. Imagine the radical transformation in the Western church if we would grasp the implications of this biblical truth!

The early church understood that church discipline was a necessary, logical consequence of their understanding of mutual accountability in the body of Christ. Jesus had clearly commanded his followers to practice church discipline:

> If another member of the church sins against you, go and point out the fault when the two of you are alone. If the member listens to you, you have regained that one. But if you are not listened to, take one or two others along with you, so that every word may be confirmed by the evidence of two or three witnesses. If the member refuses to listen to them, tell it to the church; and if the offender refuses to listen even to the church, let such a one be to you as a Gentile and a tax collector.
>
> Matthew 18:15–17 NRSV

Paul commanded the churches he planted to practice church discipline; he even spoke of it as carrying "each other's burdens" (Gal. 6:1–2). In 1 Corinthians 5, Paul demanded that the Corinthians expel from their fellowship a man who persisted in gross sin (vv. 1–5). Then he expanded the order into a general command not to eat with someone who claims to be a brother or sister in Christ but is "sexually immoral or greedy, an idolater or a slanderer, a drunkard or a swindler" (v. 11). Implementing that command today would reduce church rolls! But the Corinthians obeyed Paul and in a subsequent letter Paul urged the Corinthians to welcome back the brother who apparently had repented (2 Cor. 2:6–11).

Individualism runs deep in American evangelicalism. In a chapter titled "Democratization of Christianity and the Character of American Politics," evangelical historian Nathan Hatch shows the connection between American revivalism in the eighteenth and nineteenth centuries and the emergence of American individualism. Baptist John Leland was typical of many early American evangelical leaders. He was an anti-elitist, anti-hierarchical populist who saw the essence of Christian faith in highly individualistic terms. "Religion," Leland said, "is a matter between God and individuals."[12] What has happened, one wonders, to the biblical doctrine of the church and mutual accountability?

Recovery of the practice of church discipline in our congregations is absolutely essential if the church today is to end the scandal of cheap grace and gross disobedience. Of course, we must be careful to avoid the harshness and legalism that too often crept into church discipline in the past. But loving, firm, courageous insistence on mutual accountability must again become a normal part of congregational life. We must relearn how, as John Wesley said, "to watch over one another in love."[13]

In the Power of the Spirit

The New Testament picture of the church as a new, countercultural community living in mutual accountability and availability is truly appealing, but it's also scary and demanding. As we beg God for the grace to live it out in our time, it is crucial to remember that the early Christians never imagined that they could be this new community in their own strength. It was only in the power of the Risen Lord and the Spirit he bestowed that incarnating such sweeping change was possible.

Paul declares that believers can now fulfill "the righteous requirements of the law" because we live "according to the Spirit" (Rom. 8:4). Because the Spirit lives in us, we can say no to sin (Rom. 8:11–14). Thank God, "the Spirit helps us in our weakness" (Rom. 8:26). Therefore, Paul confidently promises, "Live by the Spirit, and you will not gratify the desires of the sinful nature" (Gal. 5:16). Truly being the body of Christ is possible only in the power of the Spirit.

Practical Steps

What concretely can we do today to recover the biblical understanding of the church as community? I want to focus on two critical areas. First, we must discover and implement practical ways to strengthen accountability in the body of Christ. That means stronger accountability structures for congregations, parachurch organizations, small groups for all church members, and a renewed practice of church discipline. Second, somehow we must dethrone mammon and materialism in our hearts and congregations through a more faithful use of our money.

The notion—and practice—of an independent congregation with no structures of accountability to the larger body of Christ is simply heretical. How can an independent "Bible church" claim to be biblical when its very refusal to submit to a larger church structure of accountability defies the essence of a biblical understanding of being the church? Being part of Christ's one body means listening to and submitting to the other parts of that body. There is simply no biblical justification for any local congregation to fail or refuse to join a wider network of churches (e.g., a denomination) that provides guidance, supervision, direction, and accountability. Nor is there biblical justification for understanding the local autonomy of the congregation within a denomination to mean that the local congregation is free to pick, choose, and ignore what the Spirit and the Word say through the larger denomination.

Second, we must find a way to strengthen mutual accountability among the myriad of parachurch organizations in the evangelical world. I know and appreciate the fact that the flexibility and creativity of new parachurch organizations have been central to the dynamic success of evangelicalism in the last half century. One need think only of the marvelous ways God has blessed the church and the world through Inter-Varsity Christian Fellowship, Youth for Christ, World Vision, the Billy Graham Evangelistic Association, and the list goes on and on. I thank God for these and thousands of others, including Evangelicals for Social Action, which I founded and lead!

But the parachurch organizations of the evangelical world have a fundamental flaw. They are autonomous organizations with almost no accountability. Anybody who can raise some money and persuade a few friends to join a board can launch a new evangelical organization. As long as they meet very minimal federal and state legal requirements, they can do anything they please. And they do! Many of the worst, most disgraceful actions that embarrass and discredit the evangelical world come from this radical autonomy.

Frankly, I do not know how to solve this problem. The Evangelical Council of Financial Accountability to which many, but not nearly all, evangelical parachurch ministries belong helps some. But we need far more accountability to the larger body of Christ. In the Roman Catholic world, the vast number of religious orders (Dominicans, Jesuits, etc.) that have emerged over the centuries are somewhat similar to evangelical parachurch organizations. They offer the same kind of creativity and flexibility in the face of new challenges. But they are accountable to the pope. I am not proposing an evangelical pope or a return to Rome. But the evangelical world must, in the next couple decades, find some new, concrete structures to provide greater account-ability for evangelical parachurch organizations.

Within the local congregation, one of the best structures for strengthening mutual accountability for individual church members is small groups. Every congregation with more than fifty members ought to establish a network of small groups in the congregation and call all its members to join one. If small groups stay together long enough, deep trust can develop and can encourage honest sharing of real struggles. Small groups can discuss major decisions that individuals and couples are contemplating: significant finan-cial choices, a potential marriage, a career change, and so on.

For a time, I was in a small group that used annual IRS tax returns to discuss the way each family spent its money.

In small groups, persons come to know each other well enough to sense when a friend is struggling in some area. Long before a marital problem escalates to contemplation of divorce, a close friend in a small group can gently ask how the marriage is going. Couples can share their struggles and ask for prayer and support.

John Wesley called this loving, caring, and accountability within small groups "watching over one another with love." Wesley insisted on tough love in small groups (he called them "class meetings"). Members asked each participant hard questions every week, including the question, Where did you sin this week? This kind of small group was at the core of Methodism during the decades that it experienced explosive growth in England and America.

Small groups do not just happen. A congregation's leaders must teach their importance and explain their theological foundation in the biblical doctrine of the church. Good small group leaders must be trained. Ongoing oversight of small group leaders is essential.[14] But when small groups work well, they offer both a powerful answer to the widespread loneliness of isolated individuals today and an effective means of mutual accountability. If all our church members belonged to a good small group, the vast majority of the struggles that eventually lead to blatant sin and the need for church discipline would be discovered and overcome long before they became visible, public problems.

Modern sociology helps us understand why small groups are so important. Sociologists like Peter Berger have explained how individuals are powerfully shaped by the "significant others" around them and the rituals and practices that we share with other members of our community.[15] Members of a group that embrace a set of ideas contrary to those of the prevailing culture find it very hard to maintain their countercultural ideas unless they enjoy strong communal bonds within the circle of those who share these divergent ideas. That, of course, is precisely the situation of biblical Christians today. Biblical values on both sex and marriage on the one hand and money and materialism on the other are radically different from those of the larger society. Daily, the larger society bombards us with TV, radio, movies, and billboards promoting its destructive but alluring ideas. It is virtually impossible, sociologically speaking, to resist these sinful values by oneself. We need intimate, ongoing fellowship in a Christian community that embraces Jesus's countercultural standards. A loving, supportive, vigorous Christian small group, rooted in a local congregation, is one of the best structures for that support.

Church discipline used to be a significant, accepted part of most evangelical traditions, whether Reformed, Methodist, Baptist, or Anabaptist. John Calvin devoted a chapter of his great systematic theology to church discipline. Calvin puts it bluntly:

> As the saving doctrine of Christ is the soul of the church, so discipline forms the ligaments which connect the members together, and keep each in its proper place. Whoever, therefore, desire either the abolition of all discipline, or obstruct its restoration, whether they act from design or inadvertency, they certainly promote the entire dissolution of the church.[16]

For centuries, Calvinist, Methodist, and Anabaptist congregations regularly practiced church discipline.

In the second half of the twentieth century, however, it has largely disappeared. Marlin Jeschke, who has written perhaps the best Anabaptist books on church discipline, quotes Haddon Robinson's summary of the current scene:

> Too often now when people join a church, they do so as consumers. If they like the product, they stay. If they do not, they leave. They can no more imagine a church disciplining them than they could a store that sells goods disciplining them. It is not the place of the seller to discipline the consumer. In our churches we have a consumer mentality.[17]

It is not surprising that a cultural setting that absolutizes consumer choice and individual autonomy has effectively pushed churches to abandon their long heritage of church discipline.

We simply must recover this biblical practice. Certainly we must do it wisely and lovingly. Too often in the past petty legalisms and harsh attitudes have crept into the process. Language about courts and trials is not appropriate. Church discipline, even the final stage of excluding persistent sinners from church membership, is really just using our last resort in pleading with an erring brother or sister to forsake sin and return to the loving arms of the Lord who longs to forgive him or her. Church discipline is finally simply watching over one another in love.

Congregations that wish to recover the practice of church discipline must start with the biblical meaning of joining the church. It is totally impossible to exercise church discipline if church members do not understand that joining this body means joining a community of mutual support and accountability, where everyone expects that other members will lovingly challenge them to more faithful discipleship. The first step is to recover the biblical doctrine of the church. The second step is to implement small group structures for mutual support and accountability. Only then is a congregation ready to practice church discipline. Fortunately, by then, if small groups are working well, most problems will be solved before they become issues requiring church discipline.

We almost certainly would strengthen the church today if we made it harder to join. For much of the first three centuries, new converts went through an extensive teaching process, finally experiencing baptism on Easter Sunday. Several decades ago, as denominations belonging to the National Council of Churches (NCC) were beginning a long, steady decline and evangelical denominations were growing, NCC staff person Dean Kelley wrote a surprising book with the title *Why Conservative Churches Are Growing*. His basic answer: they make high demands. Strong, growing churches, he argued, have clear, demanding membership requirements. Weak, declining churches do not.

Kelley pointed to the early Anabaptists and Wesleyans as excellent examples. In both instances, he pointed out, there was no hurry in taking someone into membership. Tests of membership included behavior as well as doctrine. Continuing as a member depended on continuing faithfulness. And members "made their life pilgrimage together in small groups, aiding and encouraging one another."[18]

In their study of American church life, scholars Wade Clark Roof and William McKinney reached a similar conclusion: "Almost all of the churches that retained distance from the culture by encouraging distinctive lifestyles and belief grew."[19]

I have suggested several specific ways to strengthen mutual accountability in the community of the church. These are just a beginning. In the next couple decades, our best pastors, denominational leaders, and theologians must work together to develop effective, workable, biblically faithful ways to practice mutual accountability in the church of the twenty-first century. If we do not, we can expect continuing disobedience and steady decline.

We must also dethrone mammon. I fear that many—probably most—Western Christians worship the god of materialism. If their behavior is any measure, they care more about accumulating things than obeying God. How else can we explain the fact that Christians living in the richest nation in human history give less and less to the church even though their annual incomes have increased substantially over the last three decades? Surely biblical people would have joyfully given progressively higher percentages of their income to evangelism and social ministry as they moved from unheard-of wealth in terms of all earlier periods of history to even greater, more astounding levels of material abundance. Instead, we have doubled the size of our already spacious houses and the capacity of our garages while reducing the percentage of our giving. Long ago Jesus said, "Where your treasure is, there your heart will be also" (Matt. 6:21). And evangelicals are piling up ever-greater treasures in their huge houses, growing vacation homes, and expanding investments.

How can we persuade our people to forsake this idol?

Again it must start with biblical teaching and preaching: not one evangelical pastor in ten comes even close to talking as much about the poor as the Bible does. Our evangelical preachers must correct this heretical disobedience.[20]

But words alone are not enough. Our people, especially congregational leaders, need to see poverty firsthand. Mission trips, either across town to spend a weekend with an African American or Latino congregation or to another country in Africa or Latin America, can be powerful change agents. If mission trips combine biblical teaching on the poor, careful analysis of the facts and causes of poverty, and firsthand encounters with persons experiencing wrenching poverty, people change. That kind of mission trip can transform hearts and minds. It can also produce increased giving for holistic ministry that combines evangelism and social change.

Congregations need to help individuals and families fashion specific, concrete ways to move from consumerism to sharing. I include a long list of specifics in my *Rich Christians in an Age of Hunger*. Why not start a movement of Christians who decide to use a "graduated tithe" in their giving? The more income they receive, the higher percentage they give to Christian ministry.[21] Tom Sine has promoted ideas for cohousing that would dramatically reduce the cost of housing for Christian families.[22] As we saw in chapter 1, if American Christians simply gave a tithe rather than the current one-quarter of a tithe, there would be enough *private Christian* dollars to provide basic health care and education to all the poor of the earth.[23] And we would still have an extra $60–$70 billion left over for evangelism around the world. At the very least, will wealthy Western Christians give generously to feed, clothe, and empower the tens of millions of desperately poor brothers and sisters in Christ around the world?

Think of the impact if evangelical giving to empower the poor here and abroad became so substantial that the first thought that came to secular people's minds when they heard the word "evangelical" was, "Oh, yes, they are the people who are dramatically reducing poverty around the world." Richard Lovelace and J. Edwin Orr, both evangelical historians of revival movements, point out that evangelism and concern for the poor have gone hand in hand in the great revivals of the past.[24] Dramatically expanded Christian giving to empower the poor and dedicated work to bring justice for the needy would probably provoke widespread interest in Christian faith and attract many to personal faith in Christ.

In the area of money and possessions just as surely as in the area of sex and marriage, Christians today desperately need stronger structures of mutual accountability in order to live like Jesus. Few things are more urgent than a recovery of the biblical understanding and practice of the church as community. May the head of the church empower his body to live as a caring, mutually accountable community rather than a collection of isolated lone rangers.

Rays of Hope

So be earnest, and repent. Here I am! I stand at the door
and knock.

Jesus

No biblical passage speaks as powerfully to our situation as the message to the church at Laodicea. Like
the American church today, the Laodicean church was rich,
self-confident—and lukewarm.

The city of Laodicea (in Asia Minor, now Turkey) was
famous in the first century. It was a major banking center
and proud of its wealth. The city was especially famous for
its wool exports and a highly regarded eye salve.[1] Apparently
the Laodicean church shared their fellow citizens' sense
of wealthy self-confidence. But knowing they were half-
hearted, lukewarm Christians, the Lord said to them,

I know your deeds, that you are neither cold nor hot. I wish you were either one or the other! So, because you are lukewarm—neither hot nor cold—I am about to spit you out of my mouth. You say, "I am rich; I have acquired wealth and do not need a thing." But you do not realize that you are wretched, pitiful, poor, blind and naked. I counsel you to buy from me gold refined in the fire, so you can become rich; and white clothes to wear, so you can cover your shameful nakedness; and salve to put on your eyes, so you can see.

Those whom I love I rebuke and discipline. So be earnest, and repent. Here I am! I stand at the door and knock. If anyone hears my voice and opens the door, I will come in and eat with him, and he with me.

Revelation 3:14–20

This passage could just as well have been written to contemporary American evangelicals. Enormously wealthy, and proud of it, we think that most things are going well in spite of our blatant disobedience. But our Lord's word to us is simple: Repent!

Evangelicals have used the image of Christ knocking at the heart's door as a symbol of our vigorous evangelistic programs. But in truth, it is we, by our behavior, who have excluded him from our hearts and lives. He stands at the doors of *our* hearts, begging us to welcome his total Lordship.

Weeping and repentance are the only faithful responses to the sweeping, scandalous disobedience in the evangelical world today. We have defied the Lord we claim to worship. We have disgraced his holy name by our unholy lives. Yes, we believe he is the Savior. We are Christians, not pagans. But our beliefs are not strong enough to produce righteous lifestyles. We want Jesus *and* mammon. Unless we repent, our Lord intends to spit us out.

Biblical repentance, as we saw in chapter 3, is more than a brief liturgical phrase or a hasty superficial tear. It is a deep, heartfelt sorrow for offending the Holy Sovereign of the universe and a strong inner resolve to embrace the conversion—the complete reversal of direction—that our forgiving Savior longs to bestow. We cannot manufacture this radical change using our own strength. But we can beg our Holy God not only to forgive but also to change us. Daily, we can pray to the Lord to transform us more and more into the very likeness of Jesus.

Anguished, persistent prayer for revival must become more central in evangelical life. It is true that for a couple of decades, there have been major prayer movements in the evangelical world. But our behavior has not become more holy. The revival tarries. Richard Lovelace has said that we cannot close "the sanctification gap" until "the same fear and trembling, the same prayer to be endued with power from on high that characterized the first apostles" becomes a part of our lives.[2] Please God, may that happen.

Facing the depth of the scandal could easily provoke despair. Thank God, belief in the gospel warrants a more hopeful response. At the heart of evangelical belief is the glorious biblical truth that new birth, radical transformation, is possible at any moment. We have regularly promised even the most wretched, most broken sinners that the Lord stands ready to forgive and change them if they will only open their hearts to him. Again and again, we know from our own history, the Savior has done just that. Criminals, adulterers, and murderers have been radically transformed into new persons in Christ Jesus. That is the perennial promise of the gospel.

That is precisely the promise which we must claim for ourselves. The Savior longs to forgive even scandalously unfaithful contemporary evangelicals if we will just repent.

And pray. We need to pray mightily for a sweeping movement of revival. The history of evangelical awakenings in the last three centuries shows that again and again God has responded with powerful movements of revival in the church when God's people united in intense, sustained periods of prayer.[3]

The incredible promises Jesus attached to his words about prayer strengthen our hope. If we pray for revival and sanctification, the Lord of the universe pledges to hear us. Listen to his reassuring promise:

Whatever you ask for in prayer, believe that you have received it, and it will be yours.

Mark 11:24

I tell you the truth, if you have faith as small as a mustard seed, you can say to this mountain, "Move from here to there" and it will move. Nothing will be impossible for you."

Matthew 17:20–21

If you remain in me and my words remain in you, ask whatever you wish, and it will be given you.

John 15:7

Does anyone doubt that our Lord longs to answer our pleas for revival? And sanctifying power?

As we pray, we need to remember an important condition that Christ attached to these promises. We must *obey*. John 15:7 says that Jesus will hear our prayers if we abide in him and his words abide in us. We must make every effort to embrace the righteous way of life that the New Testament commands and promises is possible.

In chapters 3 and 4, I examined what that obedience looks like. It means unconditional submission to Jesus as Lord as well as Savior. It means abandoning our one-sided, unbiblical conceptions of sin, the gospel, salvation, and conversion, and returning to the full-blown biblical understanding of these glorious truths. It means recovering the biblical reality of the church as community. It means living the truth that orthodoxy and orthopraxis—right theology and right behavior—are equally important.

If we do that, I believe we dare hope and expect that a longing for holiness will sweep through our churches. Our sexual practices will reflect biblical standards much more faithfully. Joyful, lifelong fidelity will make our homes and marriages powerful signs of an attractive alternative to today's brokenness and agony. Biblical Christians will lead the way in more vigorous efforts to reduce dramatically domestic abuse, racism, materialism, and poverty.

Could that really happen? The promise of the gospel is that it can and does—whenever people truly surrender to the biblical Christ. Fortunately, there are even some rays of hope in some of the polling data. The picture we reviewed from the data in chapter 1 is bleak and devastating. Fortunately, when pollsters make more careful distinctions between nominal Christians and devout believers, there is evidence that deeply committed Christians do live differently.

In 1992, George Gallup Jr. and Timothy Jones published a book called *The Saints Among Us*. They used a twelve-question survey to identify what they called "heroic and faithful individual" Christians. Some of the questions identified people who believed in the full authority of the Bible and practiced evangelism. But others identified costly behavior: "I do things I don't want to do because I believe it is the will of God" and "I put my religious beliefs into practice in my relations with all people regardless of their backgrounds." They labeled "saints" those who agreed with every question. And they called "super-saints" those who agreed *strongly* with every question.[4]

The good news is that the "saints" lived differently. Only 42 percent of the strongly *un*committed spent "a good deal of time" helping people in need, but 73 percent of the "saints" and 85 percent of the "super-saints" did.[5] Only 63 percent of the spiritually *un*committed reported that they would *not* object to having a neighbor of a different race. But 84 percent of the "saints" and 93 percent of the "super-saints" said they would not object.[6] Interestingly, a disproportionate share of the saints were women, African Americans, and persons earning less than $25,000 per year.

We saw in chapter 1 that sociologist Christian Smith conducted a large national poll to compare the attitudes and behavior of evangelical, fundamentalist, mainline, liberal, and Catholic Christians as well as those of the "non-religious." He found that over the previous two years, evangelicals were more than three times more likely to have given "a lot" of money to help the poor and the needy than the non-religious.[7]

In fact, evangelicals scored higher than any other Christian group. Of all evangelicals, 29 percent gave a lot. But only 23 percent of fundamentalists, 22 percent of mainline churches, 25 percent of liberals, 22 percent of Catholics, and 9 percent of the non-religious gave a lot. Even so, only 29 percent of the evangelicals gave a lot. That means 71 percent of evangelicals did not!

A Pew Center poll in 2001 supported Smith's findings. In this survey, those with a high religious commitment were a little more than three times as likely as those with a low religious commitment to have volunteered to help poor, sick, and elderly people in the last month (35 percent vs. 11 percent).[8] But again only one third (35 percent) of the highly religiously committed had volunteered. Sixty-five percent had not. Another question in the same poll found that those who were "heavily involved in activities at their church or house of worship" were almost four times more likely to volunteer to help the poor, sick, and homeless in settings outside church than were those of low religious commitment (44 percent vs. 12 percent).[9]

George Barna has developed a set of criteria to identify people with a "biblical worldview." These people believe that "the Bible is the moral standard" and also think that "absolute moral truths exist and are conveyed through the Bible." In addition, they agree with all six of the following additional beliefs: God is the all-knowing, all-powerful Creator who still rules the universe; Jesus Christ lived a sinless life; Satan is a real, living entity; salvation is a free gift, not something we can earn; every Christian has a personal responsibility to evangelize; and the Bible is totally accurate in all it teaches.

Barna's criteria for identifying people with a biblical worldview are not identical to his criteria for identifying evangelicals (see chapter 1), but they are quite similar. As we saw earlier, Barna's "born-again" category is much broader; about 40 percent of the total population are born-again, but only 7–8 percent are evangelicals. Using his definition of those with a biblical worldview, Barna has discovered that only 9 percent of all born-again adults have a biblical worldview and only 2 percent of born-again teenagers.[10] That is the bad news.

The good news is that the small circle of people with a biblical worldview demonstrate genuinely different behavior. They are nine times more likely than all the others to avoid "adult-only" material on the Internet. They are four times more likely than other Christians to boycott objectionable companies and products and twice as likely to choose intentionally not to watch a movie specifically because of its bad content. They are three times more likely than other adults not to use tobacco products and twice as likely to volunteer time to help needy people.[11] Forty-nine percent of all born-again Christians with a biblical worldview have volunteered more than an hour in the previous week to an organization serving the poor, whereas only 29 percent of born-again Christians *without* a biblical worldview and only 22 percent of non-born-again Christians have done so.[12]

In a 2000 poll Barna discovered that evangelicals are five times less likely than adults generally to report that their "career comes first."[13] And there is accumulating evidence that theologically conservative Protestant men who attend church regularly have lower rates of domestic abuse than others.[14]

Not surprisingly, this better behavior is closely corre-
lated with higher religious activity. Those with a biblical
worldview are almost twice as likely as other Christians to
read the Bible each week.[15] Nationwide, only 21 percent of
adults attend Sunday school each week, but 37 percent of all
born-again adults do. And the figure jumps to 65 percent
for evangelicals.[16] While only 20 percent of all adults attend
a small group for prayer and Bible study during the week,
28 percent of born-again Christians do. And 53 percent of
all evangelicals do.[17]

Other pollsters have discovered a similar correlation
between evangelical faith and religious activity. Christian
Smith found that evangelicals are much more likely to attend
church each week or share the gospel than other Christians.[18]
The same pattern emerged in a study in 2001 by the Pew
Research Center.[19]

These statistics offer some substantial hope. People with
a biblical worldview, and this category largely overlaps with
that of evangelical, do exhibit better moral behavior at several points. We cannot be satisfied with studies that show
that only 29 percent of all evangelicals give a lot to help
the poor and needy. But that is at least a lot better than the
statistics for the non-religious, where only 9 percent do
a lot to help the poor. When we can distinguish nominal
Christians from deeply committed, theologically orthodox
Christians, it is clear that genuine Christianity does lead to
better behavior, at least in some areas.

Barna's findings on the different behavior of Christians
with a biblical worldview underline the importance of
theology. Biblical orthodoxy does matter. One important
way to end the scandal of contemporary Christian behavior

is to work and pray fervently for the growth of orthodox theological belief in our churches.

Barna reports one final finding that offers additional hope. He discovered that even though 91 percent of all born-again Christians lack a biblical worldview, they are nonetheless open, even desirous, of spiritual growth. Eighty percent of all born-again Christians said that having a "deep, personal commitment to the Christian faith is a top priority for their future."[20] And nine out of ten Christians of every stripe said that if their churches specified things they should personally do to grow spiritually, they would at least listen to the advice and follow most of the recommendations.[21] That suggests a lot of openness to more solid biblical discipling.

Things are not quite as hopeless as they first appeared. Biblical faith makes a substantial (though not enough) difference in the lives of deeply committed Christians. Most nominal Christians seem open to spiritual growth.

More importantly, the gospel is true! The carpenter from Nazareth burst from the tomb and now reigns as the Lord of the universe. His promise to transform into his very own likeness all who truly believe in him still stands. The Holy Spirit is still alive and powerful today, radically remaking broken people who unconditionally open their hearts and lives to his mighty presence.

At any time in history, no matter how bad the current mess, no matter how unfaithful the contemporary church, God stands ready to keep his promises. God is eager to do the same mighty deeds today that he has done in the past. All we must do is trust and obey.

The Lord we claim to love and worship stands at the door and knocks. He longs to be truly invited in. We cannot invite only half of him. But if today we dare to embrace and surrender to the full biblical Christ, he will perform mighty deeds that transcend what we dare ask or imagine. He will turn our weeping into joy. He will end the scandal of blatant disobedience in the people who call on his name.

> Jesus, be the center,
> Be our source,
> Be our light, Jesus
>
> Jesus, be the center,
> Be our hope,
> Be our song, Jesus
>
> Be the fire in our hearts,
> Be the wind in our sails,
> Be the reason that we live,
> Jesus, Jesus
>
> Jesus, be our vision,
> Be our path,
> Be our guide,
> Jesus.[22]

Notes

Introduction

1. Michael Horton, "Beyond Culture Wars," *Modern Reformation* (May-June 1993), 3.
2. Alan Wolfe, *The Transformation of American Religion: How We Actually Live Our Faith* (New York: Free Press, 2003), 257.
3. Ibid., 212.
4. Tim Stafford, "The Third Coming of George Barna," *Christianity Today*, August 5, 2002, 34.
5. *Christianity Today*, October 2003, 112.
6. George Barna, *Think Like Jesus* (Nashville: Integrity, 2003), 40.

Chapter 1: The Depth of the Scandal

1. George Barna, "Family," 2000. Available from Barna Research Online, http://216.87.179/cgi-bin/pagecategory.asp?categoryid=20. See also George Barna and Mark Hatch, *Boiling Point: It Only Takes One Degree* (Ventura, CA: Regal, 2001), 42.
2. "The statistic has been quite consistent since the mid-90's." Barna and Hatch, *Boiling Point*, 42n29.

3. The Barna Group, *The Barna Update*, "Born Again Adults Less Likely to Co-Habit, Just As Likely to Divorce," August 6, 2001, http://www.barna.org/FlexPage.aspx?Page=BarnaUpdate&BarnaUpdateID=95.

4. The Barna Group, *The Barna Update*, "Annual Study Reveals America Is Spiritually Stagnant," March 5, 2001, http://www.barna.org/FlexPage.aspx?Page=BarnaUpdate&BarnaUpdateID=84.

5. The Barna Group, *Evangelical Christians*, http://www.barna.org.

6. W. Bradford Wilcox, "Conservative Protestants and the Family," in *A Public Faith: Evangelicals and Civic Engagement*, ed. Michael Cromartie (New York: Rowman and Littlefield, 2003), 63.

7. *New York Times*, May 21, 2001, A14.

8. John L. and Sylvia Ronsvalle, *The State of Church Giving Through 2001* (Champaign, IL: Empty Tomb, 2003), 12.

9. Ibid., 25.

10. The Barna Group, "Stewardship," http://www.barna.org/FlexPage.aspx?Page=Topic&TopicID=36.

11. Carmen DeNavas-Walt, Robert Cleveland, and Bruce H. Webster Jr., U.S. Census Bureau, Current Population Reports, P60-221, *Income in the United States: 2002*, (Washington, DC: U.S. Government Printing Office, 2003), available as PDF at http://www.census.gov/prod/2003pubs/p60-221.pdf.

12. Ronsvalle, *State of Church Giving*, 52.

13. Carol Bellamy, *The State of the World's Children 2001* (New York: UNICEF, 2003), 81.

14. *New York Times*, May 21, 2001, A14.

15. Lawrence K. Altman, "Study Finds That Teenage Virginity Pledges Are Rarely Kept," *New York Times*, March 10, 2004, A20.

16. The Barna Group, "Born Again Adults Less Likely to Co-Habit, Just As Likely to Divorce."

17. John C. Green, "Religion and Politics in the 1990s: Confrontations and Coalitions," in *Religion and American Politics: The 2000 Election in Context*, ed. Mark Silk (Center for the Study of Religion in Public Life, Trinity College, Hartford, CT, 2000), 21, available as PDF at http://www.trincoll.edu/depts/csrpl/religame.pdf.

18. Ibid., 26.

19. Ibid.

20. Steve Gallagher, "Devastated by Internet Porn," Pure Life Ministries, December 15, 2000, http://www.purelifeministries.org/mensarticle1.htm.

21. George Gallup Jr. and James Castelli, *The People's Religion* (New York: Macmillan, 1989), 188.

22. Personal conversation with Frank Gaebelein's daughter.

23. Bill McCartney with David Halbrook, *Sold Out: Becoming Man Enough to Make a Difference* (Nashville: Word, 1997).

24. Michael O. Emerson and Christian Smith, *Divided by Faith: Evangelical Religion and the Problem of Race in America* (New York: Oxford, 2000), 170.

25. Michael Emerson, "Faith That Separates: Evangelicals and Black-White Race Relations," in *A Public Faith* (see note 6), 196.

26. I believe in mutual submission per Ephesians 5:21. That verse 21 is the first verse of the following section is shown by the fact that verse 22 has no verb, borrowing its verb from verse 21. For excellent biblical analysis, see the many publications recommended by Christians for Biblical Equality, 122 West Franklin Avenue, Suite 218, Minneapolis, MN 55404-2451.

27. Diana R. Garland, *Family Ministry* (Downers Grove, IL: InterVarsity, 1999), 201.

28. "National Survey on Marital Strength: Executive Summary," at http://www.lifeinnovations.com.

29. Christopher G. Ellison, John P. Bartkowski, and Kristin L. Anderson, "Are There Religious Variations in Domestic Violence?" *Journal of Family Issues* 20, no. 1 (January 1999): 96, 104. Also see under chap. 5 below, n. 14.

30. Ann W. Annis and Rodger R. Rice, "A Survey of Abuse Prevalence in the Christian Reformed Church," *Journal of Religion and Abuse* 3, no. 3/4 (June 18, 2002): 17.

31. Barna and Hatch, *Boiling Point*, 140.

32. Barna, *Think Like Jesus*, 23.

33. The Barna Group, *The Barna Update*, "Surprisingly Few Adults Outside of Christianity Have Positive Views of Christians," December 3,

2002, http://www.barna.org/FlexPage.aspx?Page=BarnaUpdate&Barna
UpdateID=127.

Chapter 2: The Biblical Vision

1. Justin Martyr, *First Apology*, quoted in Peter C. Phan, *Social Thought*, vol. 20 of Message of the Fathers of the Church, ed. Thomas Halton (Wilmington: Michael Glazier, 1984), 56.

2. Aristides, quoted in Martin Hengel, *Property and Riches in the Early Church* (Philadelphia: Fortress Press, 1974), 42–43.

3. Ibid., 42–44.

4. Tertullian, *Apology 39*, quoted in Phan, *Social Thought*, 21.

5. Julian the Apostate, quoted in Stephen Neill, *A History of Christian Missions* (New York: Penguin, 1964), 37–38.

Chapter 3: Cheap Grace vs. the Whole Gospel

1. George Barna, *Christianity Today*, August 5, 2002, 35.

2. George Barna, *The State of the Church 2002* (Ventura, CA: The Barna Group, 2002), 126.

3. Peter E. Gillquist, *Why We Haven't Changed the World* (Old Tappan, NJ: Revell, 1982), 16 (Gillquist's italics).

4. Ibid., 19.

5. Ibid., 23.

6. John G. Stackhouse Jr., *Evangelical Landscapes* (Grand Rapids: Baker, 2002), 19.

7. Martin Luther, *Commentary on the Epistle to the Galatians* (Cambridge: James Clarke, 1953), 143.

8. R. T. Beckwith, G. E. Duffield, and J. I. Packer, *Across the Divide* (Abingdon, England: Marcham Manor, 1977), 58.

9. For a much longer discussion, see my *Good News and Good Works* (Grand Rapids: Baker, 1999), 52ff.

10. "The Gospel of Jesus Christ: An Evangelical Celebration," in *This We Believe*, ed. John N. Akers, John H. Armstrong, and John D. Woodbridge (Grand Rapids: Zondervan, 2000), 240, 243, 247.

11. Philip Yancey, *What's So Amazing about Grace?* (Grand Rapids: Zondervan, 1997). Yancey does not do this, but it would be fundamen-

tally unbiblical to limit grace to forgiveness. In the New Testament, the word *grace* refers to God's amazing act of forgiving us and his equally wonderful act of transforming us.

12. See *Good News and Good Works*, 95–100.

13. For the references and much more discussion, see my *Good News and Good Works*, 103ff.

14. Richard F. Lovelace, *Dynamics of Spiritual Renewal* (Downers Grove, IL: InterVarsity, 1979), 109.

15. For an extended, more careful discussion, see chap. 6 of my *Rich Christians in an Age of Hunger*, 4th ed. (Dallas: Word, 1997).

16. Cornelius Plantinga Jr., *Not the Way It's Supposed to Be: A Breviary of Sin* (Grand Rapids: Eerdmans, 1995), 12.

17. Wolfe, *The Transformation of American Religion*, 184.

18. Emerson and Smith, *Divided by Faith*, 173.

19. Ibid., 179.

20. L. Dean Allen II, "Promise Keepers and Racism: Frame Resonance as an Indicator of Organizational Validity," *Sociology of Religion* 61, no. 1 (spring 2000): 60–61.

21. This section comes from my *Good News and Good Works*, 148–51.

22. C. H. Dodd, quoted in Stephen Mott, *Biblical Ethics and Social Change* (New York: Oxford, 1982), 6.

23. C. H. Dodd, quoted in Clinton E. Arnold, *Powers of Darkness: Principalities and Powers in Paul's Letters* (Downers Grove, IL: InterVarsity, 1992), 203.

24. John Paul II, *Sollicitudo Rei Socialis*, encyclical letter, December 30, 1987, sect. 36, http://www.ewtn.com/library/ENCYC/JP2SOCIA .HTM.

25. *Christianity Today,* October 2, 2000, 40–49.

Chapter 4: Conforming to Culture or Being the Church

1. Gillquist, *Why We Haven't Changed the World*, 56–57.

2. Barna, *Think Like Jesus*, 21.

3. Gillquist, *Why We Haven't Changed the World*, 54 (Gillquist's italics).

4. Tammy Bakker with Cliff Dudley, *I Gotta Be Me* (Charlotte: New Leaf Press, 1978).

5. Robert H. Schuller, *Self-Esteem: The New Reformation* (Waco: Word, 1982), 47.

6. A case made vigorously by D. G. Hart, *Deconstructing Evangelicalism* (Grand Rapids: Baker, 2004), especially 118, 124. Hart would add the importance of Christian tradition. Agreeing with him on these points does not mean embracing his basic thesis!

7. See David Watson, *I Believe in the Church* (Grand Rapids: Eerdmans, 1978), 84.

8. Rodney Clapp, *A Peculiar People: The Church as Culture in a Post-Christian Society* (Downers Grove, IL: InterVarsity, 1996).

9. Michael Green, quoted in Tom Sine, *Mustard Seed versus McWorld* (Grand Rapids: Baker, 1999), 205.

10. Stanley Hauerwas and William H. Willimon, *Resident Aliens: Life in the Christian Colony* (Nashville: Abingdon, 1990), 12.

11. Sine, *Mustard Seed versus McWorld*, 153.

12. Nathan Hatch, "Democratization of Christianity and the Character of American Politics," in *Religion and American Politics: From the Colonial Period to the 1980s*, ed. Mark Noll (New York: Oxford, 1990), 112.

13. For an excellent book on church discipline, see Marlin Jeschke, *Discipling in the Church: Recovering a Ministry of the Gospel* (Scottdale, PA: Herald Press, 1988). See also Ronald J. Sider, "Watching Over One Another in Love," *The Other Side* 11 (May-June 1975), 10ff.; idem, "Spare the Rod and Spoil the Church," *Eternity*, October 1976, 18ff.

14. One excellent handbook on small groups is *Growth Groups* by Michael T. Dibbert and Frank B. Wichern (Grand Rapids: Zondervan, 1985). See also David Watson's *I Believe in the Church*.

15. See, for example, Peter Berger, *A Rumor of Angels* (Garden City: Anchor Books, 1970); Peter Berger and Thomas Luckman, *The Social Construction of Reality* (Garden City: Doubleday, 1956).

16. John Calvin, quoted in Eduard Thurneysen, *A Theology of Pastoral Care* (n.p.: John Knox, 1962), 32–33.

17. Haddon Robinson, quoted in Jeschke, *Discipling in the Church*, 143.

18. Dean Kelley, *Why Conservative Churches Are Growing* (New York: Harper, 1972), 125–26. For an extensive summary of the subsequent debate on Kelley's theses, see James A. Mathisen, "Tell Me Again: Why Do Churches Grow?" *Books and Culture*, May/June 2004, 18ff.

19. Wade Clark Roof and William McKinney, *American Mainline Religion* (Rutgers: Rutgers University Press, 1990), quoted in Glen H. Stassen and David P. Gushee, *Kingdom Ethics: Following Jesus in Contemporary Context* (Downers Grove, IL: InterVarsity, 2003), 489.

20. For a collection of all the biblical texts on the poor, see my *For They Shall Be Fed* (Dallas: Word, 1997).

21. See pp. 193–96 of my *Rich Christians in an Age of Hunger.*

22. See Sine, *Mustard Seed versus McWorld*, 206–9.

23. See under chap. 1 above, nn. 10, 12–13.

24. Lovelace, *Dynamics of Spiritual Renewal*, 228; J. Edwin Orr, *The Light of the Nations: Evangelical Renewal and Advance in the Nineteenth Century* (Grand Rapids: Eerdmans, 1965), chaps. 10 and 26.

Chapter 5: Rays of Hope

1. See Craig S. Keener, *The IVP Bible Background Commentary: New Testament* (Downers Grove: InterVarsity, 1993), 775.

2. Lovelace, *Dynamics of Spiritual Renewal*, 237.

3. See, for example, J. Edwin Orr, *The Eager Feet: Evangelical Awakenings, 1790–1830* (Chicago: Moody, 1975), especially 191–200.

4. George H. Gallup Jr. and Timothy Jones, *The Saints Among Us* (Harrisburg: Morehouse, 1992).

5. Ibid., 63–64.

6. Ibid., 41.

7. Christian Smith, *American Evangelicalism: Embattled and Thriving* (Chicago: University of Chicago Press, 1998), 41–42.

8. The Pew Research Center for the People and the Press, *American Views on Religion, Politics and Public Policy* (Washington, DC: Pew Research Center, 2001), 2–3; see also somewhat parallel results in Robert Wuthnow, *Acts of Compassion: Caring for Others and Helping Ourselves* (Princeton: Princeton University Press, 1991), 51.

9. Pew Research Center, *American Views on Religion, Politics and Public Policy* (2001), part IV, 5.

10. Barna, *Think Like Jesus*, 23.

11. Ibid., 24.

12. Ibid., 28.

13. The research archive on "Evangelical Christians" at www.barna .org. Here Barna reports that evangelicals are just as likely as the general population to be divorced. But in his 2002 report (*State of the Church 2002*, 94), Barna reported that evangelicals are "less likely to have experienced a divorce than any other of the faith segments." It is not clear how these different data fit together.

14. See W. Bradford Wilcox, *Soft Patriarchs, New Men: How Christianity Shapes Fathers and Husbands* (Chicago: University of Chicago Press, 2004). See also Ellison, Bartkowski, and Anderson, "Are There Religious Variations in Domestic Violence?" 96–97; Annis and Rice, "A Survey of Abuse Prevalance in the Christian Reformed Church," 19.

15. Barna, *State of the Church 2002*, 25.

16. The Barna Group, "Christian Education/Sunday School," http:// www.barna.org/FlexPage.aspx?Page=Topic&TopicID=9.

17. The Barna Group, "Small Groups," http://www.barna.org/Flex-Page.aspx?Page=Topic&TopicID=45.

18. Smith, *American Evangelicalism*, 34, 40.

19. Pew Research Center *American Views on Religion, Politics and Public Policy* (2001), part IV.

20. George Barna, *Growing True Disciples* (Ventura, CA: Issachar Resources, 2000), 32.

21. Ibid., 41.

22. Slightly adapted version of Michael Frye's song "Be the Center." Used by permission of Vineyard Music, http://www.vineyardmusic .com.

Ronald J. Sider is professor of theology, holistic ministry, and public policy as well as director of the Sider Center on Ministry and Public Policy at Palmer Theological Seminary. He is also president of Evangelicals for Social Action. A widely known evangelical speaker and writer, Sider has spoken on six continents and published twenty-seven books and scores of articles. His *Rich Christians in an Age of Hunger* was recognized by *Christianity Today* as being among the one hundred most influential religious books of the twentieth century. His most recent books are *Just Generosity: A New Vision for Overcoming Poverty in America* and *Churches That Make a Difference: Reaching Your Community with Good News and Good Works* (with Phil Olson and Heidi Unruh). Sider is publisher of *PRISM* magazine and a contributing editor for *Christianity Today* and *Sojourners*. He serves on the advisory boards of many organizations, including The Pew Forum on Religion and Public Life as well as the Faith and Service Technical Education Network of the National Crime Prevention Council. He has lectured at scores of colleges and universities around the world, including Yale, Harvard, Princeton, and Oxford.

EVANGELICALS
FOR SOCIAL ACTION

ESA is a national association of Christians dedicated to living like Jesus—living out a genuine faith in our lives and communities.

Jesus is Lord of our whole lives, and our lives must be subject to the whole of his gospel. ESA provides a network and resource for Christians committed to this kind of holistic discipleship and ministry in our lost and hurting world. Together we can share the good news of Jesus Christ through word and deed.

Join ESA and become part of an exciting movement including . . .

PRISM > ESA's bimonthly magazine will equip, empower, inform, and inspire you to live more like Jesus, growing a genuine faith in every part of your life. *PRISM* offers insightful, biblical reflection on the world in which we live—stories and strategies for effective outreach and ministry. The *PRISM ePistle*, ESA's free weekly electronic newsletter, offers timely information, commentaries, action ideas, and reviews that pertain to a whole-life faith.

Christian Citizenship > ESA helps Christians to be active, engaged, and responsible citizens. *PRISM* features a regular Washington Watch column that provides a biblical perspective on legislation coming out of the nation's capital. The *ePistle's* Public Policy channel provides reflection and discussion on current political issues.

Ministry Network > Becoming a member of ESA makes you a part of a dynamic network of Christians. Network 9:35 is our ministry networking churches and organizations committed to the kind of faith-inspired holistic life (teaching, preaching, and healing) described in Matthew 9:35.

Caring for Creation > ESA hosts the Evangelical Environmental Network (EEN), an association of Christian organizations that make care for creation an integral part of their work. World Vision, Habitat for Humanity, and InterVarsity Christian Fellowship are among the members of the environmental network. EEN also produces *Creation Care* magazine, a biblical quarterly on the environment.

Join Us!

Evangelicals for Social Action • 10 Lancaster Avenue • Wynnewood, PA 19096
1-800-650-6600 • esa@esa-online.org

ESA is affiliated with The Sider Center on Ministry & Public Policy at Eastern University

Is your *church* meeting all the needs of your *community*?

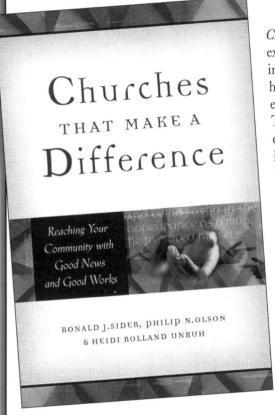

Churches That Make a Difference explores the how-to's of developing and maintaining an effective holistic ministry that combines evangelism and social outreach. The authors draw on extensive experience with church ministries and faith-based organizations as they share the life-changing vision and biblical mandate for living the whole gospel. This comprehensive resource will give you and your church concrete ways to pursue holistic ministry in your community.

"This is compulsive reading because it's not a set of ideas but realities that have been worked out in the ministry of local churches. I wholeheartedly commend it."
—**Clive Calver**
president, World Relief

ISBN 0-8010-9133-0
$19.99p

BakerBooks
Relevant. Intelligent. Engaging.

www.bakerbooks.com